Amitav Ghosh's Writings

Issues, Ideologies and Craftsmanship

Amitav Ghosh's Writings

Issues, Ideologies and Craftsmanship

Bhakti Vaishnav

ATLANTIC

PUBLISHERS & DISTRIBUTORS (P) LTD

Published by
ATLANTIC
PUBLISHERS & DISTRIBUTORS (P) LTD
7/22, Ansari Road, Darya Ganj, New Delhi-110002
Phones : +91-11-40775252, 23273880, 23275880, 23280451
Fax : +91-11-23285873
Web : www.atlanticbooks.com
E-mail : orders@atlanticbooks.com

Branch Office
5, Nallathambi Street, Wallajah Road, Chennai-600002
Phones : +91-44-64611085, 32413319
E-mail : chennai@atlanticbooks.com

Printed in India at Nice Printing Press, A-33/3A, Site-IV, Industrial Area, Sahibabad, Ghaziabad, U.P.

Dedicated to

Asmita, Dharmik, Nishchint words are insufficient to speak, yet I wish to say thank you. Heartfelt thanks to Dr. Sanjay Mukherjee, Dr. A.K. Singh, Dr. Kamal Mehta and all the teachers at Department of English, Saurashtra University.

Foreword

The novel, in its relatively short generic history, has become the most important literary document claiming a near-independent epistemological space of its own. Since its early days it has been that literary genre which has continuously resisted the stamp of the fictive on itself although the material text happily donned the publishers' category of Fiction. And throughout the twentieth century it has consistently maintained via myriad narratological techniques of spatiotemporal play a 'truth seeking' character (if I may borrow this phrase from Iris Murdoch, who in her life—while she taught philosophy at Oxford pondering, as philosophers are wont to do, over the truth-untruth dyad—achieved the stupendous feat of writing twenty-six novels), at the same time enchantingly mystifying and defamiliarizing fact and history. And in this fleet-footed peregrination over the last century, the novel has, without abandoning the prerogative of a free subjective voice, most significantly and effectively, become political.

The subaltern voice (and by Shiva, it can now speak!), has at least one more perspective to offer, and I use the term 'subaltern' here in its broadest sense of subordination and concomitant marginalization, one that has found its use in the works of writers of the First World too. I am especially reminded of a poem, "A Subaltern's Love Song", which is rich in its tonality and self-consciousness, and is written by John Betjeman, who, while writing the poem from a junior army officer's point-of-view (literally, a subaltern), knew that English poetry on a 'love song' after T.S. Eliot would forever remain a subaltern piece of work. But the extra dimension in a subaltern work I mention is in the sense elaborated by Edward Said in Orientalism where, remembering Antonio Gramsci he reiterates the fact that only a subaltern subject can write about what it means to be a subaltern, and an inventory of that consciousness is never available to the agency that has deliberately perpetrated the othering. Amitav Ghosh, who for a while was associated formally with the Subaltern Studies Group contributing an essay—"The Slave of H.M.S. 6"—to the *Subaltern Studies* volumes (by Oxford University Press), brings into his works the meticulous research of a social anthropologist, an economist and a new historicist, the gripping storyteller in him (my favourites still are *The Shadow Lines*, *The Calcutta Chromosome* and *The Hungry Tide*—constituting as I like to think, his Bengal trilogy) always alert to how a simple, forgettable character is caught between the cross-currents of and impinged by history. It is these characters that become Ghosh's protagonists from his earliest Aloo to his latest Deeti who attempt—often in vain—to steer their frail vessels through the vicious political drifts of clashing cultures. And in the process, Ghosh's tales open up long forgotten (or deliberately suppressed) narratives that qualify as counter-discourses like the one in his latest trilogy on the opium trade route in early nineteenth century colonial India fully sanctioned by the Raj when most people today only retain facts about indigo, sugarcane or cotton plantations during the British rule because details of the latter as official agricultural activity—orchestrated and foregrounded instead of their coffers filling up through cultivation of large tracts of poppy plants—presented a more benign face of colonization, like in our own times the American invasion of Iraq ostensibly to rid the world of a nuclear threat was a crude façade for retaining supremacy in the global oil trade. That the governing ideologies in our own postcolonial and imperial times are similarly Janus-faced is but one of the intellectual enjoyments we derive reading Amitav Ghosh, as the writer of this book, *Amitav Ghosh's Writings: Issues, Ideologies and Craftsmanship* has endeavoured to uncover through her critical study quite commendably.

It is a matter of singular satisfaction for a teacher when a student ventures out beyond the pale of the conventional curriculum to realize his/her own potential and dare to forge an identity in the domain of higher education to find a calling in teaching-learning and research. I have known Ms. Bhakti Vaishnav since her early diffident and hesitant student days, a decade and a half ago, when she entered the university where I teach. Discursive-analytical issues always interested her, and with her penchant for reading, willingness to gather exposure and the subsequent increase in her level of confidence, she began to discover her area of interest in the interface between literature and the socio-cultural and metaphysical realms of inquiry. Thus, she veered into reading Amitav Ghosh and decided to work on his works for her doctoral research. Sincerity and a striving for proper academic standards in criticism and research have been desirable and debatable issues for almost a century now since the establishment of English Studies (as we know it now) at Cambridge. The readers of this text would not find dearth of these qualities here. I invite them to embark upon a stimulating reading about perhaps the most exciting Indian English novelist writing to unearth untold or prohibited truths today.

Sanjay Mukherjee
Department of English & CLS,
Saurashtra University, Rajkot, India

Preface

In the evolution of the novels written in English as a literary genre in India, the works of first generation writers generally show a great concern about national and social problems. The novels of the 1960s have a private tone focusing on an individual's life, and are introspective in structure. The novels from 1980 onwards, however, have created a watershed in the history of Indian English fiction as they have brought a significant change in the world view, expression and the form. Distinctly, Amitav Ghosh, through his writings, throws a challenge against the age-old way of thinking in which reason and logic hardly find place.

Amitav's writings bring forward his deep insight into historical events as well as human behaviour. Anti-colonial spirit, for example, is reflected in his *The Glass Palace*, and *The Shadow Lines* is against artificial international borders. Similarly, out of conviction, he has written *The Calcutta Chromosome* with a view to undoing the Western sense of superiority, vis-à-vis touching their monopoly over the scientific research. Here he comes out as an extensive experimentalist for whom ideas are the vital driving force.

The book puts Ghosh's ideology in a perspective of the "Circle of Reason" through context and history as Ghosh himself neither indulges in India bashing to encash sympathy from the West, nor does he glorify it by romanticizing its exotic aspect under the garb of "the essence of India". It deeply touches upon the relevance of the issues taken by Ghosh in his fiction and non-fiction, and his contribution to Indian Writing in English in terms of intellectual and literary debates. The readers will find the book very interesting, educative and thought-provoking.

Bhakti Vaishnav

Contents

1

Context

(I)

The evolution of the novel written in English, as a form, in India has been described by Meenakshi Mukherjee in the following words:

> the birth and the development of the novel in India as genre nursed by, if not born out of the tension between opposing systems of values in a colonial society, and modified by certain indigenous pressures. (*Realism and Reality: The Novel and Society in India*, Meenakshi Mukherjee (1985))

The growth of novel, like any other art form in the nation has been greatly influenced by the issues and environs of independent India. In fact, Indian English novel reflects the rising nationalism and has grown with the nation's independence. The novels by the first generation writers show concern with national and social problems. The novels of the 1960s have a private tone focusing on an individual's life and are introspective. Novels from 1980 onwards created a watershed in the history of Indian English novels as they brought in a significant change in the world view, expression and the form.

The novels of Mulk Raj Anand reflect nationalism, social concerns, and Gandhian and Nehruvian socialism. Anand's novels are recognized as an instrument to see the history of Indian novel in English. His experiments with social realism and the exuberance of North Indian dialects, laid the foundation for linguistic and cultural representations in future novels. The classic foreword to *Kanthapura*[1] has been recognized as a manifesto for the path Raja Rao had opted and preached for Indian Writing in English. He resolved the dichotomy of foreign (English) language and methods of Indian storytelling tradition through a systematic indigenisation of English and a spirit and tempo of Indian life. He deviated from the sacrosanct structure of European novel and shaped it on the lines of the epic tradition of India. He complemented Anand's effort of introducing North India to Indian English novels by bringing in an unusual blend of South Indian—French cultural vistas and realities. R.K. Narayan has seen himself 'as realistic fiction writer' [Mishra, Mehrotra (ed.) 195]. He focused on the anxieties, disappointments and struggles of a generation who stood on the threshold of independence, the point where the institutions established during British Raj were still dominating and negotiating their way into independent India. Aubrey Menon is an important figure who has been marginalized in the discussion of the novels during and after independence. With an added advantage of his complex cultural background, he portrayed an objective view of East and the West. He beholds a mirror to the world and gives his insight on the all pervasive system of injustice and hypocrisy, racism, the tension between so-called 'civilised' and 'primitive' people and various aspects of colonialism through his fictional and non-fictional writings. Again often oversighted in the history of Indian English novels, *All About H. Hatter* is a guiding milestone. G.V. Desani broke away with the rules of grammar and diction of standard English and adapted the Joycean style for language in this novel. Structured around seven episodes which are subdivided further into 'Digest', 'Instruction', 'Presumption' and 'Life Encounter'. *Hatter* as a novel set the stage for Rushdie's *Midnight's Children* with unpunctuated sentences and random capitalization.

The great trio of Mulk Raj Anand, Raja Rao and R.K. Narayan had been penning down fiction in English before and after independence. However, writing fiction in English was not explored much by larger groups of authors in India during this period. In fact, for almost two decades after independence, the exercise of writing a novel in English was considered against the norms of loyalty for the nation. It took more than ten years for a novel in English to receive Sahitya Akademi award. R.K. Narayan's *Guide* heralded the era of acceptance of English novels by Indian authors as an indigenous genre by winning the Sahitya Akademi award in 1960. Indian English novel also marched ahead with the general economic growth and prosperity sustaining the temporary setbacks of war and loss of great leaders.

Indian writers in English in the 1950s and 1960s were concerned about character development, psychological depth and an effort to negotiate the sense of alienation in the modern world, albeit, the nature of both 'alienation' and 'modernity' were not the same for India as it was for the West. The emergence of women novelists was a significant development of these decades. Writers like Kamala Markandaya, Ruth Prawer Jhabwala (for the reason she has accepted the fact that her novels are written on India), Nayantara Sahgal and Anita Desai came upon the stage and shared the platform enjoyed by the best known writers in English. These women writers of the first generation engaged themselves with issues of women in conventional marriage systems, human relationships, and contemporary social and political developments from a woman's point of view along with the psychological influences of contemporary world. The novels of these years exhibited a command over the form but lacked innovations. As Shyamala Narayan and Jon Mee point out, except one or two examples,

> None of the books of this period,...are interested in developing the conflict between tradition and modernity which are a thematic feature of so many of their stories—into any kind of formal exploration of indigenous narrative forms. [Narayan and Jon Mee, A.K. Mehrotra (ed.) 230]

Nevertheless, several major Indian English novels were published during the 1960s. The titles produced during this span of twenty years include: *The Serpent and The Rope*, *The Cat and Shakespeare*, *The Guide*, *The Man Eater of Malgudi*, *Sunlight on a Broken Column*, *A Bend in the Ganges*, *Storm in Chandigarh*, *A Handful of Rice*, *Nectar in a Sieve*, *Bye Bye Black Bird*, *Cry, The Peacock*. There was no huge spurt of creativity or production during 1970s. Economic decline, War and Emergency disturbed the nation during this time. The effect of the same was reflected through a very thin stream of creativity. This period remains as a memory lane where the writers of the next generation would visit and revisit.

The publication of *Midnight's Children* in 1981 is considered to be a harbinger of renaissance in Indian Writing in English. Certain elements of postmodernism, play with language and grammar, focus on history, liveliness of language, innovations through magic realism and allegory, references to contemporary Hindi cinema all made a smooth entry to the world of Indian English novel with Rushdie's highly influential novel. The writers after 1980 have shown a skillful mastery of the form and innovations. They gave shape to the thematic aspect of conflict between tradition and modernity and resolved it through innovation in stylistics. Commercial development of publishing Indian language within India also played a vital role in boosting the zest for writing fictions in English. Jon Mee points out an interesting fact, "To attribute everything to a single, personal intervention would be naïve" [Mee, Mehrotra (ed.) 318].

He points out the fact that the reading of the accounts of the origins of I. Allan Sealy's first novel, *The Trotter Nama*, "if Rushdie ushered in a new era of Indian Writing in English, it has to be acknowledged that he was more a sign of the time than their creator" [Mee, Mehrotra (ed.) 319].

A combination of postmodern vision and continuation of narrative techniques of Indian epic tradition is a distinct feature of novels published after 1980. This generation of authors were relieved off the burden of the co-consciousness of both English language and novel as a form as something that belonged to the West. These novelists use English language deftly, covering a larger canvass of emotional, political, cultural, geographical and historical issues. There is an awareness of national and international developments reflected in themes woven around the displaced, marginalized modern man and uninhibited modifications in the genre. There is a gusto of creativity, vigor, hope and confidence surfacing through rich, mischievous language, light-sometimes funny, comic and humorous approach that reigns their writing. Novels like *Midnight's Children*, *The Golden Gate*, *The Circle of Reason*, *Plan for Departure*, *The Great Indian Novel* are a few examples of the same.

Thus, to sum up, one can say looking back in history of novel writing in English in India after 1930s, the great trio of Mulk Raj Anand, Raja Rao and R.K. Narayan based their stories on different themes like the freedom struggle, Gandhian ideology and its impact on society, need for social reforms, eradication of social evils, India's modern destiny, the Partition, the emergence of the new urban India, the problems of rural India, etc. The second generation writers like Nayantara Sahgal, Manohar Malgonkar, Khushwant Singh and Bhabani Bhattacharya emerged by the 1960s and their writings added a new direction to fiction with new subjects, though there was a lack of proliferation during this time. Nayantara Sahgal took up the political theme, Manohar Malgonkar explored historical perspective by portraying the upheavals of his time. Arun Joshi and Anita Desai ushered in the era of psychological fiction. Khushwant Singh depicted the suffering of people during the holocaust of the Indian Partition. By the 1980s, the novel flourished and advanced in themes, use of language, style and technique. Writers like Salman Rushdie, Rohinton Mistry, Amitav Ghosh, Shashi Tharoor, Arundhati Roy, Vikram Seth, have set their premise of writings around various socio-political and cultural issues that emerged in post-independent India and rapidly changing Indian life; the socio-political, cultural issues of a young multicultural democratic nation and their impact on communities and an individual's life. Salman Rushdie ushered Indian Writing in English in a new and improvised era of a fine balance of craftsmanship, innovation and ideological issues. Shashi Tharoor captured the political scenario while Rohinton Mistry focused on the scams in banks when banks in India underwent transformation and were getting nationalized and the impact of the same on Parsi community. Vikram Chandra furthered these explorations by chronicling Indian history from about 1750 to 1900. These post-colonial, post-partition Indian authors learned this history in its aftermath, and now craft stories of India and her history with exceptional skill and remarkable artistry.

(II)

The era of the so-called 'phase of post-modern novel' for Indian English novel has also uncovered a conundrum of debates and dialogues. Rushdie initiated the contested idea of advantageous position of a migrant writer in the post-modern world. Both his works and opinions kindled favorable response towards multi-culturalism overshadowing and undermining the voices and writings of the native writers. Simultaneously, it is important to look at the question that has bothered all Indian writers and critics in all Indian languages—the question of capturing the true essence of Indianness and that too in English. Meenakshi Mukherjee brought up the issue of the often overlooked plurality of India. She pointed out the fact that the exponents of Indianness sometimes overlook the multi-lingual, multi-racial and multi-religious nature of the country. Again some of the prevalent characteristics of the post-modern and post-colonial style are not something that was introduced to Indian writers for the first time. The cultural consciousness of the country has seen the higher level of representation of heterogeneous culture and varieties of narrative techniques explored to the fullest. However, during the upswing of the post-colonial debate the narrative techniques and the writers were being perceived through a different glass. Critics like Edward Said and Homi Bhabha deliberated on the subject of hybridity and cosmopolitan writers. The term 'cosmopolitan writers' was exclusively meant for migrant writers. The plethora of novels that capitalized on the name of diaspora writing, cosmopolitan world view against imperialism, going beyond myopic nationalism by the self-assumed role of representatives of the Third World amongst First World intellectual is undeniable. Critics like Aijaz Ahmad, Timothy Brennan and Revati Krishnaswamy have countered the views on post-colonial and post-modern approach. They have shown a dissent with the First World post-colonial writers and academicians for providing undue privilege to the works of migrant writers over non-migrant writers. Critics like Arif Dirlik and Aijaz Ahmad have defied the theoretical and intellectual activities that lack references to everyday sociality. Furthering the discussion, Arif Dirlik in his article titled "Postcolonial Aura: Third World Criticism in the Age of Global Capitalism" argues, "The predominantly epistemological and psychic orientations of postcolonial intellectuals are ethically incompatible with and irrelevant to the problems of social, political and cultural domination" [Dirlik (quoted from) Leela Gandhi 331].

The debate bases itself on the age-old question of mimetic form and the relationship between theory, practice and criticism. But as Leela Gandhi points out, "Taken to extreme, the unilateral privileging of experience over theory—or activism over academy —works to disqualify or debar the social validity of almost all intellectual activity" (Gandhi 61).

Concurrent to these arguments on cosmopolitan writers and native writers, was the debate and endless discussions on post-colonial theoretical positions. Post-nationalist school of thought tried to bridge the divide between the native and the colonizer. Theoreticians were concerned with the principle of two objectives: (i) it endeavoured to show the mutual transformation of the coloniser and the colonised emanating from the cultural encounter, and (ii) an inter-civilisational alliance against institutions of oppression and universal suffering. The debates and conditions of contemporary world have also influenced these post-colonial/post-modern writers. The three conditions described by Leela Gandhi are:

> a growing body of academic work on globalisation insists that in the face of the economic and electronic homogenization of the globe, national boundaries are redundant or—at least—no longer sustainable. The random flow of global capital is accompanied...by an unprecedented movement of peoples, technologies and information across previously impermeable borders. The resultant condition of first two is forced contiguity or overlap between diverse and mutually antagonistic national histories. (Gandhi 125-26)

Thus, it is the rapid development of various theories and conditions that played a chief role in cultivating a world view and practice of contemporary Indian authors. The generation that embarked upon literary journey after *Midnight's Children* have chosen their issues and ideologies with a conscious knowledge of the intellectual, economical, political and traditional implications of fictional writing in English. The fresh breeze heralded by these literary writers of Indian novelists in English, has brought in new life to the state of relative quietude that prevailed in Indian Writing in English under colonization.

Referring to the argument of Indian novels in English after 1980 as post-modern novels, one must pay attention to the socio-cultural and religious differences that exist between Indian society and the West during the era of post-modernism. Thus, the writers of English novels from India after 1980s have been influenced by Gabriel Marquez, Vargas Llosa, Milan Kundera, etc. but their works have been shaped by their view of India. The characteristics described by Bernnan to describe the practice of post-modernism by the Third World writers include: (1) disgressions and juxtapositions, (2) humorous parody of current and identifiable villains, (3) novel as history of present—a vehicle of information conveying the urgency of the historical record for those in dominant culture, (4) feeling that art glories in the realization of its functional role in political and social life, (5) tradition, popular roots, (6) quotations from high culture and effort to popularize the same. This list is misleading as except the second feature about parody, all other characteristics can be traced in the novels published before independence. They are present even in *Kanthapura* penned by the first generation writer Raja Rao and published in 1938. However, for the engagement with theories on deconstructive, postcolonial and feminist theories, indulgence in fragmentation, magic realism, statements on metropolitan views, plurality and depiction of subaltern issues, issues of subjectivity and identity, intertextuality, humour and rapid change influencing human existence place novels after *Midnight's Children* along with the best of the contemporary literary writings.

(III)

> By a curious paradox, the room for dissent has shrunk as the world has grown more free, and today, in this diminished space, every utterance begins to turn in on

> itself. This, I believe, is why we need to recreate, expand, and reimagine the space for articulate, humane and creative dissent. (Ghosh 2002: 285)

As clear from the above lines, Amitav Ghosh takes the role of a writer with a conscious responsibility. Unlike others, Salman Rushdie and Amitav Ghosh have remained consistent and prolific since their arrival in the literary world. Rushdie introduced new narrative techniques and innovative use of language along with a novel subject. Revealing a deep influence of Rushdie in *Circle of Reason*, Ghosh matures gradually in a unique style of his own with the growth of his works. He continues to be a strong voice among contemporary literary artists and thinkers for both his fictional and non-fictional writings. He has carved out a unique niche for himself by embracing new genres, styles and subjects. He cannot be categorized or confined within the boundaries of any typical genre and he belongs to the world of novels and non-fictional prose. He has emerged as a prominent writer with the force of sheer verisimilitude and versatility. Besides this, a vast range of characters lends a quality of cosmopolitanism to his subject. His issues are local and global at the same time making the themes universal. His oeuvre is marked with the traits of interdisciplinarity and postmodernity; continuous innovation and occupation with a variety of subjects.

Amitav Ghosh was born in Calcutta on July 11, 1956. His father's job as an army officer and later as a diplomat provided him with an opportunity to spend his formative years in India, Iran, Sri Lanka and East Pakistan. He attended the Doon School in Dehradun and received a BA in history from St. Stephen's College; the alma matter of several other writers like Shashi Tharoor at Delhi. He received his master's degree in Sociology from Delhi University in 1978. Then he proceeded to acquire a diploma in Arabic from Tunisia and his Doctorate in social anthropology from Oxford University in 1982. He has been a visiting Professor at many universities like the University of Virginia, Centre for Social Sciences at Trivandrum, the University of Virginia, University of Pennsylvania, American University in Cairo, Columbia University and continues to be a distinguished

Professor of Comparative Literature at Queen's College of the City University of New York.

Amitav Ghosh made his literary debut with the *Circle of Reason* in 1986. The very first novel was hailed by the critics as a remarkable technical achievement. He was awarded with Sahitya Akademi Award for his second novel *The Shadow Lines* (1988). He also received Anand Purskar for the same novel. He has also received many other prestigious awards like Pushcart Prize, Grand Prize for fiction and Arthur C. Clark Award, presented to the best science fiction in 1997 for *The Calcutta Chromosome* (1996). His non-fiction writings have also received no less appreciation. *An Antique Land* (1992) was named as one of the notable books of 1993 by the *New York Times*. He was also nominated for the American Society of Magazine Editor's Award for reporting for *Countdown* (1999). *Dancing in Cambodia and at Large in Burma* (1998) brought travel, history, cultural commentary and political reportage gelling into one seamless essay. *The Imam and The Indian* (2002) a collection of 18 essays addressing different issues like fundamentalism, history of novel, Egyptian culture, literary awards in Third World was written over a span of 16 years from 1986 to 2002. These essays were written during the gaps between his novels, thus, providing a track record of the evolution of the author's interest and ideas for fiction. A recipient of Padma Shree, Ghosh has received the esteemed Grinzane Cavour Prize for his contribution to the world of literature. *Glass Palace* (2000) and *Hungry Tide* (2002) were received with accolades carving a more respectful niche for Ghosh. He has launched his ambitious *Ibis* trilogy with *Sea of Poppies* in the year 2008. The second part of the trilogy *River of Smoke* has also been published in June 2011.

The discussion on the awards and accolades entails an incident that provides an insight into Ghosh's ideology. In 2001, *Glass Palace* was nominated for the Commonwealth Writer's Prize. Ghosh requested for the withdrawal of the book from the competition. This reaction stirred up a vortex of controversy but it effectively cleared the slightest of the doubts on his stand as a writer and regionalism. In his note requesting the withdrawal, he writes,

> The phrase itself—commonwealth writers anchor an area of contemporary writing not within the realities of present day, not within the possibilities of future, but rather within a disputed aspect of past. It seems to me that 'the Commonwealth' can only be a misnomer so long as it excludes the many languages that sustain the cultural and literary lives (of the countries that are member states). (Ghosh PEN: 35)

As a trained anthropologist and researcher, long association with subaltern studies group, with an experience of journalism and academics in both the West and in India. Ghosh overcomes the issues raised against the categories of migrant and native writers of India. The issues of subaltern world and the contemporary issues in South Asian countries, imperialism, and subtle reflection of political, economical and cultural materialism are interlaced with his ideological opinions. Interdisciplinarity, Plurality of individual's existence and continuous play of centre and margin; all these qualities mark his writing as writing in the Derridean tradition.

Ghosh has told Sheela Reddy that his fictions have always been about, "communities coming unmade or remaking themselves... the backdrop is wide but the focus is on an individual. He further opines that the focus has to be an individual or else when you hold up a mirror to violence, all you see is more violence"—John Hawley comments,

> an ambiguous but suggestive phrase, arguably emphasizing the individual as the important locus for change. He is obviously clearing a space in his definition of his writing so that the term for what he does happily include anthropology, historical research, fiction, social commentary, and—in a word—the freedom to invent new forms. (Hawley 166)

Ghosh has clearly shown indignation with the debates on Indian languages versus English debates worded his opinion in the Literary Festival at Delhi in 2002. Rukmini Nair writes, "(Ghosh)...seemed impatient with these gripes.... A writer's business was to write, and problematic values could, in his view, be interrogated effectively through English as through any other Indian language" [Nair (ed.) 165].

Ghosh neither indulges in India bashing to encash sympathy from the West nor does he glorify India by romanticizing exotic aspect of India under the garb of 'the essence of India'. Though a cosmopolitan writer, if judged by the myopic criterion, Ghosh prefers to be known as a writer belonging to the other less glamorous and internationally underplayed category of Indian writer.

Ghosh has chosen a category for himself and declared it in a talk with Sundeep Dougal,

> I think of myself as an Indian writer in the first instance. By this I mean that my work has its roots in the experience of the people of the Indian sub-continent, at home and abroad. I think I would be uncomfortable with any categorization of my work that did not acknowledge this. In this sense, 'Indian Writing in English' seems to me to be a perfectly acceptable categorization of my work. (Dougal, qtd. from Hawley 169)

He weaves his stories using various strands of imagination, history, politics and economics. All his characters and events, though imaginary, are created around some facts from the past or present. For him, the characters and stories have to be rooted in the solid soil of reality of human life. His writings penetrate through various forms and institutions of power in society and seek to comprehend human existence in totality. Power structures have always prevailed and controlled an individual's life. The interest of Ghosh lies in etching out the life of characters who would have lived or are living through such power structures enduring the unpredictable scheme of Time. Few remain alive on the memory of rapid and swarming tides of accounts of human life and survival. Selected events, individuals and sufferings remain central and get noticed. It is Ghosh's effort to sketch the other aspects that are seldom the focus of these accounts, he makes an effort to put forward the argument that these events or individuals did not or do not exist in isolation. These unheard, unseen and unaccounted events, individuals and sufferings are

Ghosh's base for the story to be structured. With reference to the context mentioned above, the book aims at studying the following aspects in Amitav Ghosh's writings:

- The relevance of the issues taken up by Ghosh in his fiction and non-fiction.
- Subaltern issues and subaltern characters in his works.
- The skillful enmesh of history in his writings and his approach to history and historicism.
- The intricate relationship of issues, ideology of the author with his craftsmanship.
- His ideological positions as reflected through the salient features of his narrative.
- His contribution to Indian Writing in English in terms of intellectual and literary debates of post-colonial/ post-modern world.

Thus, the book is an attempt to show how Amitav Ghosh's writings endeavour creatively to negotiate through the complex web of historical, political, economic and cultural issues, past and contemporary, and through his craftsmanship emerge a certain ideology on subaltern issues and his stand on national and global historical events which are not only interesting but also contribution to the world of literature.

The book studies his approach towards history and historicism in the following chapter. New historicism and postcolonial debates have charted out a subaltern study as a new area of study for people who explore and retrieve marginalized voices. The chapter on Kaleidoscopic views on subaltern examines Amitav Ghosh's engagement with the issues and life of an individual's life from the point of view subaltern studies and his unique way of combining the theory into practice. Amitav Ghosh combines his ideological positions and the narrative techniques skillfully in his writings. This aspect is studied in the Chapter 4 "Confluence of Ideology and Narrative Craftmanship". The last chapter emphasizes the fact that Ghosh's writings are imbued with his concerns for history and subaltern. Thus, his writings are the examples of artistic expressions of the ideological concerns of the world as it is and as it was.

Note

1. Foreword (*Kanthapura*)

   There is no village in India, however mean, that has not a rich *shala-purana*, or legendary history, of its own. Some god or god-like hero has passed by the village—Rama might have rested under this pipal-tree, Sita might have dried her clothes, after her bath, on this yellow stone, or the Mahatma himself, on one of his many pilgrimages through the country, might have slept in this hut, the low one by the village gate. In this way, the past mingles with the present, and the gods mingle with men to make the repertory of your grandmother always bright. One such story from the contemporary annals of my village I have tried to tell. The telling has not been easy. One has to convey in a language that is not one's own the spirit that is one's own. One has to convey the various shades and omissions of a certain thought-movement that looks maltreated in an alien language. I use the word 'alien', yet English is not really an alien language to us. It is the language of our intellectual make-up. We are all instinctively bilingual, many of us writing in our own language and in English. We cannot write like the English. We should not. We cannot write only as Indians. We have grown to look at the large world as part of us. Our method of expression therefore has to be a dialect which will some day prove to be as distinctive and colourful as the Irish or the American. Time alone will justify it. After language the next problem is that of style. The tempo of Indian life must be infused into our English expression, even as the tempo of American or Irish life has gone into the making of theirs. We, in India, think quickly, we talk quickly, and when we move we move quickly. There must be something in the sun of India that makes us rush and tumble and run on. And our paths are paths interminable. The *Mahabharata* has 214,778 verses and the *Ramayana* 48,000. Puranas there are endless and innumerable. We have neither punctuation nor the treacherous 'ats' and 'ons' to bother us—we tell the interminable tale. Episode follows episode, and when our thoughts stop our breath stops, and we move on to another thought. This was and still is the ordinary style of our story-telling. I have tried to follow it myself in this story. It may have been told of an evening, when as the dusk falls, and through the sudden quiet, lights leap up in house after house, and stretching her bedding on the veranda, a grandmother might have told you, newcomer, the sad tale of her village. Raja Rao mentions, Nov. 1937 Kanthapura (the name of the village)—the story of how the Gandhian struggle for independence came to one small Indian village in south India. Narrated by an old woman inhabitant, it evokes the spirit of India's traditional epics, the puranas and the nationalist upsurge fusing with religious faith and conflict.

2

History and Historicism in His Works

> The past, as Faulkner famously said, is not over, in fact the past is not even the past. One of the paradoxes of history is that it is impossible to draw a chart of the past without imagining a map of the present and future. History, in other words, is never innocent of teleologies, implicit or otherwise...the actions of the state provide that essential element of continuity that makes time, as a collective experience, thinkable by linking the past, the present and the future. The state as thus conceived is not merely an apparatus of rule but 'a conscious, ethical institution', an instrument designed to conquer the 'unhistorical power of time'. (Ghosh 2002: 318-19)

With the advent of post-modernism and deconstruction, history as the History was not only challenged but replaced, renegotiated and revised. The endlessness of openness and impossibility of closure in a discourse toppled the authority of history. History, too, like other disciplines underwent a sea change in the second half of the twentieth century. The thinkers questioned the discipline because the failure of a comprehensive history was quite evident. The discourses and theories that emerged as a production of various reactions accept the failure of historical (re)presentations and celebrates the possibilities of interpretive accounts, problematisations, uncertainties and dilemmas whisked out of the calm surfaces of the history.

Intrinsic qualities of history such as historical facts, structures, periods, meanings, documents became just other extrinsic ascriptions. Now, it is accepted as a fact that nobody has a patent on the past as history that dominates is always an end-product of endless appropriations. Michael de Certeau has put forward an argument that says that all history is really historiography and is always self-referencing in terms of its own credibility. The aporic world of interpretation and pluralism makes a way for 'traces' to be explored. This play in interpretation has become more enticing when applied to literature which is believed to be an interpretation and criticism of life.

Webster's Unabridged Dictionary defines historicism as (1) a theory that history is determined by immutable laws and not by human agency, (2) a theory that all cultural phenomena are historically determined and that historians must study each period without imposing any personal or absolute value system, (3) a profound or excessive respect for historical institutions, as laws or traditions, (4) a search for laws of historical evolution that would explain and predict historical phenomena. (Random House: *Webster's Unabridged Dictionary*, E version.)

History, in broad sense, stands for a study or record of past events. Historicism is

> in critical discourse suggest either that human thought is historically grounded and undergoes epistemological transformations during the course of history or that history is understood as a teleological process, wherby transformations occur as part of general and necessary series of developments. (Wolfreys et al. 42)

As an aspect of literary criticism, historicism seeks to study literary work in its heterogeneous contexts. It recognizes the fact that a literary work permeates social, historical and cultural forces of its era in its composition. The introduction of new ideas and new theories in twentieth century led to questioning of the authority and authenticity of historians and history itself.

New historicism emerged in North America and became prominent in 1980s. This approach politicized the issue and critically examines the intricate relationship of literature, culture and history. New historicism, defies the concept of history as a developing totality, a seamless overarching unity, instead they attempt to see history as a shifting and contradictory representation of numerous 'histories'. They are more concerned with the multiple and contradictory material practices which are embedded in historical events. The social contexts are seen as narrative constructions produced through the manipulations and relationships of power.

> While rejecting the overarching models of analysis, new historicism addressed the question of text and history not as a relationship of text and context or foreground and background, but instead insisted on an understanding of the text as a privileged monument within a network of discursive and material praxes.... While interests among new historicists are wide ranging, what is arguably typical of the new historicist analysis is the focus in the reading of the text on the ways in which a text produces a subversive critique of dominant ideologies from the period in which it is produced, only to find that subversion ultimately recuperated and contained by the conservative powers against which it has sought to and articulate itself. (Wolfreys et al. 124-25)

Roland Barthes in his *The Discourse of History* demonstrated that facts were linguistic entities. For Barthes, historians perform a sort of magic whereby what is just a discursive concept—'the facts'—are projected into a realm supposedly outside of discourse from which they can be thought to determine the very discourse which posits them as facts in the first place. This is not to deny the actuality of past happenings, but only to argue that they do not count until they are given significance in discourse. Chris Lorenz also suggests that reality is a form of description and therefore a perspective. For him, it is always a historian's perception of the facts that shape up the history. Thus, he pointed out the overlooked aspect of influence of an individual's subjectivity. By showing the example of discourse on nationalism in *Historical Knowledge and Historical Reality*, he proves that there is no guarantee of consensus in history. It is now accepted that the so-called past could not exist meaningfully on its own. It was pliant and lacked the form, it has always been the prerogative of the historians to mould the facts and give it a proper structure and shape.

Hayden White has also voiced similar reservations for history. He defied the authority or possibility of single viewpoint for history. He also established the force and effect of an individual's perception and interpretation that can play with the facts. He added one more dimension of individual's capacity for creativity and imagination. Therefore, the element of fiction also prevails in the narrative of history. He brought out two aspects of narrative history from the point of view of subjective influence.

(i) There cannot be a single point of view of history

(ii) Element of fiction is an intrinsic part of narrative history.

Thus, there cannot be 'The History' or History as 'The Truth'. Hayden White took it as axiomatic that histories—especially narrative histories (though probably all histories are narratives in their overall structures) are basically fictive. That is to say, though historians may wish to tell the truth and nothing but the truth about their objects of study and about that they glean for archive, they cannot narrate their findings without resort to figurative discourse.

In this context, Ankersmit said, "We can say the simula cra(text) precedes reality...that history is as much 'made' as 'found'"—coinciding with Hayden White's definition of history as "a narrative discourse the content of which is as much imagined as found" (Ankersmit 98).

It is this argument which leads Ankersmit to his idea of histories as proposals; as presentations and not as re-presentations. Thus, a historian puts forward what he thinks of an event as a presentation and proposes the facts to be reality. The entire debate on the authenticity of history and exclusive nature of the hegemony has opened up new avenues to explore the realms of marginal discourses. As an attempt to bridge the gap and to derive the missing links of the totality new historicists have accepted the presence of 'other' facts from the past. The question of how to repair the elisions of this unhistorical historiography, remains a challenge and an opportunity as well. Guha says, "by recuperating, recognizing, recovering multiple stories from non-elite, subjugated, subaltern pasts" (Guha 21). Critical theory of history tries to examine the rules of writing history and seek hidden part of history. The theorists are in argument that for hundreds of years of misinterpretation by historians was an instrument to manipulate future. On the other hand, "The fact that the historian's empirical account and the novelist's imaginary story share the narrative form...has challenged thoughtful students of imaginative literature and of history since Aristotle" (Burner 45).

History is again a 'story' of people of particular time in past. The authenticity of these documentations is always under skeptical criticism. We know what happened during an event but know it partially, as it tends to generalize and bring in the major threads of the fabric. Even generalised statements about such events overlook and the victims or the people who suffer because of such events, they get quantified and get reduced to numbers. For example, we say that 50,000 Jews were killed during Nazi regime, we just know the numbers not the lives. Here is an endeavour by Ghosh to imagine and create those situations from history and see what happens to an individual life when he/she is part of historical events. Some authors in Indian Writing in English have explored this dynamic world of theories and have reveled in this conjecture resultant of a mishmash of theories and literature. The focus is shifted to what history does not say. This gap of what is not being said becomes the foreground for practical imagination for some of the authors like Amitav Ghosh who continuously through fiction and non-fiction endevour to establish a link between the past and the present. His canvass is filled with an amazing merger of real and fiction from history and present. Enmeshing history and literature is not an unfamiliar territory in Indian literary tradition. It is the tradition that has borne epics like *Ramayan* and *Mahabharat* that have survived for hundreds of years as history, mythology and literary masterpieces. It is noteworthy that Indian writers in English such as Rushdie and Ghosh are well conversant with the issues and debates on history/historicism and historiography as well as India's tradition of narrative.

In an Antique Land is a book based on Amitav Ghosh's research on twelfth-century merchant Abrahim Ben Yiju and his servant Bomma simultaneously narrating the author's experiences at Egypt while conducting the investigation for the research. It was in 1978 when Amitav Ghosh chanced upon the letters that referred to the master and the slave of twelfth century. The first of these letters was written in 1148 in Aden, by a person named Khalaf in Ishaq. The letter reveals that Ben Yiju lived in south India at Mangalore to be precise, at that point of time. This time is also remarkable from the point of world history as it was the same time when Damascus was encircled by a large army of crusaders. The slave of the letters was not mentioned until the same letters came to the notice of the scholars, ironically these letters were written nine years earlier than the first letter that triggered attention from the scholars like E. Strauss. Various papers of Ben Yiju, a Jewish merchant from Tunisia were discovered centuries later in a synagogue in Cairo. His slave is described as Ben Yiju's Indian slave who was also a respected member of his household. This sets the premise for the various possible threads of histories Ghosh weaves in his stories and demonstrates a pattern in which the past gets connected to the present. He engages himself with the history of people and the place they belong to.

History of a place is always filled in with people's stories. The versions of these stories may differ but the crux of these stories reveals a place's growth and its people's long journey with time. It also indicates the intricate relationship of their past with their present condition. He narrates the history of old Cairo in *In an Antique Land*. He begins with the etymology of the original name 'Masr' which means 'to settle' or 'to civilise' and then shows us the transformation of the word Miisr to Egypt. With this linguistic evolution and transformation of the word, we are also acquainted with the fact and manner in which Egypt has been described, perceived and represented by Christian Europe.

While describing Babylon, he goes back to history which also reveals various stories/theories about the name of the place. Looking at the desolate condition of the fortress, he says:

> Incredible as it may seem, this putrefying pit marks the site of what was perhaps the single most important event in the history of Cairo, indeed of Egypt; it was thought to have effeted his entry into Babylon in 641 AD—the decisive event in the Fustat, the Muslim victory over the Christian powers Masr. (Ghosh 1992: 35)

The legend of Amr, the invasion by Jawahar the Greek in 969 AD, stories about the foundation of the township of al-Qahira, medieval Fustat, the glorious time during the Fatimid Empire, the present state of ruins of Babylon and Fustat all demonstrate a history of decay and regeneration of Masr. Thus, we know about the glorious past of place that lies in ruins. The rubbish dump of Fustat, like many other places across the world stands as a representative of the fact that the cultures move on and the vary places that were the locus of a particular civilization loses its glory and sheen with time.

The story of the slave also highlights the history of the synagogue of Ben Ezra. The reason for constructing a Geniza—a storehouse of records, documents, manuscripts and books within a synagogue was to eliminate possibilities of disrespect to God because the written word was considered to be holy. The Geniza of the synagogue at Ben Ezra was rebuilt in 1025 AD. The accumulated documents in the Geniza were a wide range right from manuscripts, letters, business, agreements, books and even divorce records written in Bombay which dates back to 1875 all were dumped inside it for more than eight centuries. Ghosh, then, picks up the history of Geniza from the time which he describes as "Egyptomania". The beginning of intellectual colonization of Egypt is described as follows:

> Unknown to herself, she was already on her way to becoming a victim of the enlightenment's conceptions of knowledge and discovery. In fact, the first detailed plan for the conquest of Egypt was conceived not by a soldier but by a philosopher, Karl Liebnz as early as 1870. (Ghosh 1992: 82)

The Geniza came under a closer scrutiny and attracted more attention from the Europe from 1864 onwards with frequent visits by Jacob Saphir. His visits were the inspiration for scholars like Paul Kahle, Elkan Adler, Dr. Solomon Schechter. Dr. Schechter, we are informed, was the key player in transporting the heritage that lay in Geniza to Cambridge University. The Chief Rabbi at Cairo had allowed the entire heritage to move out without realizing the actual value of the papers of Geniza.

It also adds another dimension of the fact of a parallel history of a culture within a dominant culture. The history of the travel of Geniza also remained unnoticed as the prime Islamic culture of Masr never paid attention to the parallel history of Jewish presence in Egypt which Geniza housed within itself. Referring to the history of the Jews, he also appreciates the fact that Masr was the place that had preserved Jewish history for almost a thousand years, whereas the countries that had carried away the documents would have surely destroyed them had they been lying in their limits during that period of history. He aptly says,

> The irony is that for most part they which had sustained the countries which would have long since destroyed the Geniza had it been a part of their own history. Now it was Masr, which had sustained the Geniza for almost a millennium, that was left with no traces of its riches: not a single scrap or shred of papers to remind her of that aspect of her past. It was as though the borders that were to divide Palestine several decades later had already been drawn, through time rather than territory to allocate a choice of Histories. (Ghosh 1992: 95)

The time span covered in this book begins with the time of the Crusades and ends with the Gulf War. The collection of stories, beliefs, events, insights into history entwines vivid history of Egypt, India and the culture of medieval Jews, Muslims and Hindus in the two countries.

Synchronic and diachronic approach is the source for the reconstruction of slave's story in *In an Antique Land*. Thus, his book also tries to reconstruct various aspects of history and histories of related aspects while narrating the story of Ben Yiju, specially his life in India.

Mangalore of medieval times too is reconstructed for our eyes with the details on mercantile activities and international trade on the shores of the place. With the help of contemporary traveler's observations, the author describes the rich town as a premier port: blessed with industrial crafts and richest spice producing territories of the medieval world. The story of Bomma is situated in twelfth century but the history of the place is traced back to first century with reference to its political history. He also mentions the facts mentioned by Ptolemy, the Alexandrian geographer for the land of Alvas as Mangalore was known at that point of time. Derivations of historical facts through other sources including literature are also mentioned. He also gives account of Akadevi and other poets which gives an idea of contemporary socio-religious beliefs.

"Human Tragedy in Cairo", "Petrofication" and "Empire and Soul" all these essays capture one or the other component of history. 'History of Novel' also talks about, the history of the novels in the author's uncle's house. During his childhood, Ghosh used to read from the collection that was there in his family house. At the time of writing this essay as a grown up and a professional author, he describes the physical transition of the collection and derives an understanding on how such a wide range of such great authors had been selected by his uncle. He tries to probe into the factors that affected the purchase of novels during that period.

'The Diaspora in Indian Culture' traces the inherent relationship between the cultural and political context of Indian diaspora and V.S. Naipaul's work, between modern India and its diasporic population. He also mentions the distinct nature of diaspora in Indian culture. Other cultures like Greek, Turkish or Anglo-Saxon migrations of recent history that replicated their political and social institutions hence the relationship between diasporic populations and their mother countries were continued, though partially. But in case of India it doesn't show any such continuity of institutional relationship. He also differentiates the nature of diaspora with reference to language. He says, "India exported with her population, not a language, as other civilizations have done, but a linguistic process—the process of adaptation to heteroglossia" (Ghosh 2002: 246).

After establishing the distinctive nature of Indian diasporas in West Indies, Fiji, Mauritius, Guyana, the Gulf, South Africa, he says,

> The relationship between India and diaspora is very peculiar, almost inexplicable phenomenon...the relationship is a genuine historical anomaly: in the first place because we have to recognize that the links are not those of language, religion, politics or economics. In a sense the links are those of culture, but again of a kind of culture in which the most important cultural institutions as we usually understand them—for example, language and religion—are absent. (Ghosh 2002: 247)

History also records the changes and chronology of events. Literature need not necessarily record the changes in chronological manner—but represents such changes. Ghosh represents the changes that take place at individual level and at national and international levels. Thus, his representation encompasses both micro and macro levels. He uses the mirror of time to reflect images of changing times.

The visible change in people's lifestyle and attitude, specially the ones who reside in small village of Nashaway due to faster means of communication and easy access to information gleams brightly towards the end of *In an Antique Land*. The author also observes a remarkable change in people's attitude.

> Everywhere in Egypt people seemed talking of killing.... Never before in Egypt, had I heard ordinary people so much as criticise their president in public, amongst strangers, far less talk of killing him, even if metaphorically. (Ghosh 1992: 39)

History of a place is again an intricate layer for *Hungry Tide* too. Nirmal unfolds the history of settlement at Lusibari and other places nearby, developed by Hamilton to Kanai, the young boy. History is again a leitmotif in *Hungry Tide*. Talking about the larger historical memories, Nirmal says,

> Why anyone should know or remember this: yet in the tide country, where life was lived on the margins of greater events, it was useful also to be reminded that no place was so remote as to escape the flood of history. (Ghosh 2004: 77)

Ghosh tries to capture the events and puts Sundarbans, a remote and unnoticed place, afloat on the flood of history. It is noteworthy that due to the rising concern about the ecology, Sundarbans has caught attention now but it remained silent for years together.

It is also noteworthy that there are two approaches to historiography in his writings: one is fiction through history and second is history through fiction. History of research on the Malaria bug is the base on which the entire fictional work of *The Calcutta Chromosome* is constructed. *The Glass Palace* and *Sea of Poppies* are stories that unfold aspects of colonization of Burma, Indian settlement in Burma, history of exploitation of natural resources in Burma, Mandalay, the exodus of Indians from Rangoon, the thriving trade of Afeen by Britishers in India that led to the Opium Wars. In fact, all his works interweave history and fiction in a manner that is inseparable and at the same time not compromising either of the two.

In *Countdown*, he goes to the village near Pokharan, the site of nuclear tests. Meeting with the villagers, the youngman, the clerk who refuses to give his name all become live documents for the historical moment of the nuclear tests that took place and its understated negative effects in the surrounding villages.

History as a narrative of experiences of individuals is also an interesting aspect of his approach to history. What was the effect on individual's life during Pol Pot's regime? What was it during dancers' visit to France? Ghosh tries to answer these questions. *Dancing in Cambodia* is a collection of his meetings with individuals who have survived Pot Pol's regime. Moyaka—a mid-level civil servant, Chea Samy—the veteran classical dancer, Loth Sieri—one of the brothers of Saloth Star, Khieu Seng Kim—a journalist turned into a restorer and a teacher in the department of archeology, the monk in Angkor Wat, Kong Sarith—a student turned into a guide all reveal unique stories of survival through hunger, suffering and death of the loved ones. They all become memoirs that Ghosh uses to document individuals' real stories that create histories within the sweeping phase of a larger historical event. The author also meets the family members of Pot Pol. This allows him to sketch the image of the tyrant with words. He describes the emotional experience of his mother on the night when he did not return and she was able to understand the meaning of it. Ghosh's meeting with Pol Pot's sister-in-law, again, traces the history of Pol Pot's entry into the palace, his education at France, his affinity with political leaders back home and the evolution of a communist tyrant. This help us see the evolution of a child into a ruthless leader who was born and brought up in a country that had a colonized king and gets exposed to the liberal thinking of the West. The combination of this acquired knowledge and contemporary political scenario in and around Cambodia gave birth to his ugly dream and his ambition. The interviews here are subtle, the author leaves it upon the reader to derive the inferences and develop an insight.

He also refers to the accounts of Eva Mysliwiec, who had worked for relief amongst Camobodians. Her memories of that time is marked with sudden and volcanic outbursts by people. Those people would suddenly start describing what they had seen and lived through which also included memories of a brother called away in the dark to be shot dead, infants beaten against trees, children starved to death in mother's lap. All such unlivable things that they would have put aside during their camp lives would resurface in their minds as if a camera unfolding the reel. While describing the account of Moyaka, Ghosh says that he had heard many such accounts specially from women wherein they had build their houses gradually by picking up the rubbles together. He says,

> They had lived through an experience very nearly unique in human history: they had found themselves adrift in the ruins of society which had collapsed into a formless heap, its scaffolding systematically dismantled, picked apart with the tools of murderously rational form of social science. (Ghosh 1998: 17-18)

The account on Cambodia begins with a description of Dance in France in 1906 and ends with a dance performed in 1988. The turbulence between the two dances is an experience of torment, death, suffering and vices. There are three dances the book is concerned with. One is the classical dance that was performed by the royal troupe of Burma which enthralled Marseilles in the past. The second is the metaphoric dance of cruelty, suffering and death during Khemer Rouge Regime and the third is the performance by the trained dancers in Phenom Penh in 1988 which the author describes as 'a moment of epiphany' (Ghosh 1998: 51). This performance was marked by the spirit of affirmation to life. Amitav Ghosh reflects, "It was a kind of rebirth: a moment when the grief of survival became indistinguishable from the joy of living" (Ghosh 1998: 52).

Dance stands for the heritage, the glorious past. Dancing together again has multiple meanings and effects. It stands for hope, unity of the community, a sense of celebration, joy of coming together, more importantly it gives a sense of strength, and peace of mind. Here it also stands for resurgence, reassurance and renewal. Dance has always been an integral part of all cultures. It expresses the emotions and philosophy of a culture. This dance is in sharp contrast with the dance of death, deconstruction and decay during the Pol Pot's regime.

This can be called a reflective history in a loose sense. Here such paroxysms speak for the intensity of the experience. He stands between the slices of time and tries to understand the predicament of humanity. History is a narrative in which he combines growth and regression, nobility and vice, suppression and resilience. The insight that we derive from Ghosh's account of Cambodian history is disturbing. It is again an account of a point in history that stands for the fact that how humanity suffers if the human ambitions and thinking take a brutal form and manifests itself in power. This also shows the uglier aspects of power play that prevailed even after the fall of Pol Pot.

The Shadow Lines also covers two major historical events, one the World War II in distant past from the time the novel is situated and second is the communal riots in 1984. The backdrop of the bombings in world war is not so much explored as the event of communal riots in 1984. This event is a very important point in the plot of the novel as Tridib is killed by an angry mob during the riot. The novel also sketches an individual's memories during the historical period of growing Indian nationalism through grandmother's stories of her youth. The events like partition, riots which became events of national trauma is brought to us as experiences of individuals who lived through them or suffered through these events. He says, "I was determined now that I would not let my past vanish without a trace; I was determined to persuade (others) of its importance" (Ghosh 1988: 217).

Reflecting on the connection between his memories and its evolution into fictions, Ghosh says:

> *The Circle of Reason* had grown upwards, like a sapling rising from the soil of my immediate experience. The *Shadow Lines* had its opening planted in present, but it grew downwards, into the soil, like a root system straining to find a source of nourishment. It was in this process that I came to examine the ways in which my own life had been affected by civil violence. I remembered stories my mother had told me about the Great Calcutta Killing of 1946; I remembered my uncle's stories of anti-Indian riots in Rangoon in 1930 and 1938. At the heart of the book, however, was an event that had occurred in Dhaka in 1964, the year before my family moved to Colombo: in the unlit depths of my memory there stirred a recollection of a night when our house, flooded with refugees, was besieged by an angry mob. I had not thought of this event in decades, but after 1984 it began to haunt me.... I went to libraries and sifted through hundreds of newspapers and in the end, through perseverance, luck and guesswork I did find out what had happened. The riots of my memory were not local affair: they had engulfed much of the subcontinent. (Ghosh 2002: 315)

The flow of time is also expressed by the images of various historical places and sites. Tridib's fascination for ruins and the current state of Angkor Wat, references to historical monuments of Calcutta in *The Calcutta Chromosome*, references of botanical gardens in *The Hungry Tide* and *Sea of Poppies*, the fall of the king's palace in *The Glass Palace* all these represent the change that takes place along with the sweeps of history and how ruins stand as relics of historical legacies. "Stories in Stones" open up a thread of history that connect Cambodia of past to its present. The temple of Angkor Wat was built by the King Suryavarman with a belief to be received by gods after his death. Ghosh questions the established fact of so-called discovery of the temple in nineteenth century by French explorer Henri Mouhot. The practice of performing rites by Buddhist monks had continued during the period when Angkor Wat remained under the shadow. The building stands as an example of continuity of traditions through history withstanding the times of decline. As such "monuments are usually absorbed into living history" what Mr. Mouhot would have discovered was a discovery for themselves. Ghosh points out the irony in the entire situation where the discovery is actually discovering the discoverer. The author also criticizes the efforts of restoration that mainly seem to be an effort of displacement of the living tradition of the place. Criticizing all such efforts, he says, "The story is a familiar one, for in this century many other parts of the world have seen their present being technologically and symbolically superseded by the relics of their past" (Ghosh 1998: 60).

New Historicism takes the basic argument of semiology—that the meaning of a sign can only be explained with reference to the systematic relations which it hides—and scales it up into a principle for a whole discourse. Ghosh's writings also explain an individual's life with reference to the systems in which an individual is placed. The situations in Cambodia and Burma can only be understood wholly with reference to things which have slipped off in past. These situations, like a sign, stand for many unspoken, unwritten and unnoticed facts. Ghosh projects such situations in fictions and non-fictions too. He brings the intricate relationship of historical, political and social aspects as systems that are often indiscernible in the structured discourses on society. This also reveals his views on the elusive nature of history and process of selection and exclusion in writing history. Similar view is also presented by contemporary writers like Julian

Barnes. He sums up the complexity of the issue in a nutshell in *A Sense of Ending* in following words, a character speaks:

> Indeed, isn't the whole business of ascribing responsibility a kind of cop-out? We want to blame an individual so that everyone else is exculpated or we blame a historical process as a way of exonerating individuals. Or it's all anarchic chaos, with the same consequences. It seems to me that there is—was—a chain of individual responsibilities, all of which were necessary, but not so long a chain that everybody can simply blame everyone else. But of course, my desire to ascribe responsibility might be more a reflection of my own cast of mind than a fair analysis of what happened. That's one of the central problems of history isn't it sir? The question of subjective versus objective interpretation, the fact that we need to know the history of the historian in order to understand the version that is being put in front of us. (Barnes 12)

The discussion here goes on to debate history as "lies of the victors 'against' a self delusions of the defeated" (Barnes 16). This debate is concluded on a note that "History is that certainty produced at the point where the imperfections of memory meet the inadequacies of documentation" (Barnes 17).

It is again a unique technique of introducing the debate of the world of theory in fiction. Thus, literature becomes a representative of dominant cultural and theoretical debates. Thus, complex issue of history, historiography and historicism is also dealt by many other contemporary writers.

Ghosh has expressed his own view on his concentration on history in the following words:

> My essential interest is in people and their lives, histories and their predicaments. If history is of interest to me it is because it provides instances of unusual and extraordinary predicaments. For instance, take Arjun at the battle of Jitra (*The Glass Palace*): his life is brought to crisis by a historical circumstance. He shares this circumstance with many others, but he responds to it in a fashion that is particular to himself. This crisis is more dramatic than any

> I could have thought up on my own, and that is why it is so rewarding to look at history carefully. (Hawley 6)

A.N. Kaul has criticized Ghosh's novel for being too willing to privilege imagination over history. His criticism is relevant to some of his fictional works. However, it is equally important to take note of the discussion in the beginning of the chapter, the proportion of facts and imagination is always under scrutiny even for history. As a writer, Ghosh tries to represent some incidents from the time before now. His non-fictional works are accounts of real life events and real characters whereas in fiction, the situations are all based on real events, he peoples it with imaginary characters.

Historical events are intrinsic part of Ghosh's oeuvre. He dwells into the history of the subjects in his fictional as well as non-fictional works. He scrutinizes present turmoil as a result of past. He also examines the influence of past on present and reveals the predicament of individuals who are subjected to the events of history, individuals who do not appear in the spectrum of history but the ones whose life underwent a complete transformation because of the larger political, social and national upheavals. Continuing with his style, he equates both the present and past of Burma. Two pasts of Cambodia too, are being juxtaposed in this account: one distant past filled with glory and glamour, immediate past destructive, disturbing present. While describing historical visit, he uses the newspaper report to authenticate his picture.

He focuses more on the personal lives against the backdrop of massive historical sweeps such as wars and riots, the downfall and exploitation of Burma in which also includes world war and the subject nations during these devastating years, Afeen Wars, the suffering before, after and during, Pol Pot's regime, specially the wreckage caused by Khmer Rouge movement and military rule and fragmentation of Burma in the twentieth century, the violence and destruction in Sri Lanka, Mughal King Babur's life and time, the history and politics involved in the announcement of literary awards to non-Western authors. Historical events are always the background against which all individuals lives revolve in all novels. *The Shadow Lines* continuously revolves around partition, riots and flittingly refers to the World War II. *The Calcutta Chromosome* is anchored on the history of malaria research in India. *The Glass Palace* captures events of British invasion on Burma, partition and the great exodus. *The Hungry Tide* refers to the history of settlement in Sundarbans and Sir Daniel Hamilton's intervention in it. *Sea of Poppies* is set in the background of the great opium trade and the author promises to bring in the Opium War in the following parts of the trilogy. It becomes a world of stories of individuals who have/could have/would have lived through such times and would have suffered, prospered or doomed during those events. Such stories capture various hues in which various events manifested in lives of contemporary individuals.

Ghosh sets the stage, peoples it with fascinating characters, and then rather broadly interprets the play as paradigmatic of similar events throughout history. As Ghosh recounts his tale of past events, he takes us to the time in which he personally enters the historical chain of events. His interest in history and a rich mixture of facts and fiction are so intense that the reader visits and revisits the places and events. Meenakshi Mukherjee sums up her appreciation for his skilled representation of the past in following words: "Other histories and other geographies come alive and align with our own through Ghosh's transculent prose" (qtd. from Hawley 6).

The situations and the characters intend to highlight the universality of experience. They could have been soldiers like Arjun who would have found themselves caught in the net of crisis, equally realistic is the character of Rajkumar who lands in Burma as an orphan and exploits the situation to his favour throughout his life, a lady like Kusum could have lived amongst the refugees in Sunderbans, people like Deeti and Kalua would have traveled far in order to save themselves from the oppressive clutches of society and live a respectable life; each character and every situation evoked in his fictional works are realistic. Ghosh builds them on the lines of probability and possibilities on the basis of facts derived from his study of a particular event. The result of these researched aspects of past is not an improbable fantasy but a work of imagination. It is an embodiment of research and creativity. *The Calcutta Chromosome* is one such work where he lets his imagination take a higher flight and the story travels through the realms of possibilities stretched to extremes.

One important aspect of history is evolution of human beings through science and technology. *The Calcutta Chromosome* talks about history of research on Malaria, *The Circle of Reason* talks about history of phrenology in a rather tongue in cheek manner, *The Hungry Tide* narrates the history of scientific study on Irrawaddy Dolphin in South Asia, *Sea of Poppies* describes the history of studies and research in Botany in Calcutta. As a literary writer, he uses his licenses to explore historical events on the lines of possibilities and probabilities.

Retrieving past from archives is one instrument of new historicism and subaltern studies. The much celebrated essay on 'The Slave of Ms H6' recovers an anonymous individual from medieval time. Amitav Ghosh puts the pieces of his life and his world together on the basis of the letters and documents available in library. Here, while mentioning the plurality of information provided by these documents he also words the possibilities of history that archives can yield in the following words:

> Each of these documents has a story of its own; of travel from Aden and Egypt, to Malabar and Sicily and then back again to Cairo-medieval histories that dispersal in modern times. *Their history has the baffling elusiveness of lights seen in parallel mirrors; they are both the stuff of history and history itself, as real as a battle or a temple; they are each a living history and a commentary on the writing of history; a mocking aside on histories are stolen, bought and traded in the marketplace.* (Ghosh 2002: 179, emphasis added)

As discussed above, the practice of recreating history is omnipresent in his fictional works too. Even the blurb of the latest fiction *The River of Smoke* promises such practice in the themes and one of the excerpts published in the newspaper describes Behram's encounter with Napolean. Ghosh has acknowledged that he reconstructed this scene on the basis of a letter he had found in the archives that described an unknown individual's encounter with Napolean.

Ghosh engages personal reminiscence to replicate the workings of memory in 'remembered' histories. He focuses on memory of public events in private memory, which colours and distorts them in accordance with personal biases and priorities. It is used by Ghosh to call attention to the selective nature of recorded history of Indian nationalism and exclusion of all that was not in line with mainstream narrative. The story of grandmother about her classmate, who was an active member of an extremist group stand for the unsung freedom fighters who chose the other path for freedom fighting.

As Prof. John Arnold sums up:

> Social history has been transformed from history... with the politics taken out (as the British historian G.M. Travelyn once described it) to a lively, argumentative and powerful field, combining the insights of Marxism, anthropology, sociology and annaliste mentalite to produce an understanding of the everyday lives of past people, and how these lives combine to affect 'what really happened'. It should be clear by now that actions, of the general populace have just as much to do with 'big' events as decisions made by a small group of elite kings, politicians and rulers. (Arnold 114)

Thus, Ghosh captures history with all its complexities. There are multiple ways in which he engages history and aspects of historicism/new historicism as an intrinsic aspect of his works. The myriad manners of this engagement are as following:

- Meets people and documents individual's history also documents it as an individual's story in fiction.
- Narrates history while visiting places.
- Juxtaposes present and past—a recurrent element of fiction and non-fiction.
- Past restructured on the basis of documents, building up on traces.

- Weaves history both in syntagmetic and diachronic manner in fiction and non-fiction.
- Even fictional works are wrapped in historical garbs. He fictionalizes out of facts—historical events. The list of documents and archives he acknowledges in his works are proofs of his fictions being imbued in history. Based on historical data available, he poses some histories of the people whose lives and voices are never a part of history. This is an attempt to write subaltern history through fiction and making the theory into practice in a unique manner.

3

Kaleidoscopic View of 'The Subaltern'

Random House online defines Subaltern as following:

1. Lower in rank; subordinate: a subaltern employee.
2. British Military: noting a commissioned officer below the rank of captain.
3. (In Logic) denoting the relation of one proposition to another when the first proposition is implied by the second but the second is not applied by the first.
4. (In Aristotelian logic) denoting the relation of a particular proposition to a universal proposition having the same subject, predicate and quality.
5. Of or pertaining to a proposition having either of the relations to another.

The term subaltern comes from the word 'subalternus'. The word consists of Sub means 'under' + alternus which means "every other, one after the other". The term is believed to have assumed the meaning "a person of inferior rank", as the designation in army, from 1680s (http://www.etymonline.com). The term 'subaltern' was used with additional nuance by Antonio Gramsci in his essay "On the Margins of History" during the regime of Fascist censorship. The concept was more popular amongst theorists as it could represent the lack of agency that was still present in the term 'proletariat' of Marxism. The theory that evolved around the concept of 'subaltern' meandered through extreme debates regarding this agency and ability. Gayatri Chakrabory Spivak has consistently used the term 'subaltern' to base her theory of postcolonialism. Spivak used the term to describe the lower layers of colonial and postcolonial society. She has also made it clear that this generalization is made with a conscious knowledge that the subaltern subject is irretrievably heterogeneous. Questioning the method in which marginalized are slumped together she says,

> The *antre* of situational indeterminacy these careful historians presuppose as they grapple with the question, Can the subaltern speak? *Taken as a whole and in the abstract* this...category...was heterogenous in its compostition and, thanks to the uneven character of regional economic and social developments, *differed from area to area*. The same class or element which was dominant in one area... could be among the dominated in another. This could and did create many ambiguities in attitudes and alliances, especially among the lowest strata of the rural gentry, impoverished landlords, rich peasants and upper-middle peasants all of whom belonged, *ideally speaking*, to the category of "people" or "subaltern classes". (Spivak 80)

A group of intellectuals in India established Subaltern Studies Group and used this term as an anchor to base their endeavour of identifying a mode of historical practices that survived through colonialism.

Furthering the discourse of subaltern and the role of subalterns, the Subaltern Studies Group set to seek modes of historical practices that try to restore an indigenous culture which it believes to be impervious by colonialism. In his Introduction to the first volume, Ranjit Guha declares the agenda,

> Parallel to the domain of elite politics there existed throughout the colonial period another domain of Indian politics in which the principal actors were not the dominant groups of the indigenous society or the colonial authorities but the subaltern classes.... This was an autonomous domain.... Far from being destroyed or rendered virtually ineffective...it continued to operate vigorously...adjusting itself to the conditions prevailing under the Raj. (Guha 30)

It is an arduous task to perceive the heterogeneity that was carpeted by the hegemony of the powerful. Amitav Ghosh was also a member of the same group. His essay "The Slave of Ms. H6" was written for *Subaltern Studies: Writing on Asian History and Society*. Amitav Ghosh's association with Subaltern Studies Group is quite evident in his works as well.

As a writer, Ghosh negotiates with this challenge in an integrated manner that synthesizes the matter, subject and the issues. He employs two methods to incorporate the discourse of subaltern writings. Firstly, his writings, both fiction and non-fiction become the central stage for the characters who belong to the group of marginalized. Secondly, the stories and issues are construed as a representation of the issues of subaltern class.

The larger canvass of any event tends to overlook an individual's experience during the massive sweeps of historical, social or political upheaval. As a token representation, sometimes the liberal accounts take one or two cases from the group that dwell on margin when it comes to bearing the brunt of change. Ghosh plays with this concept of centrality of role and brings the marginalized into centre by making it their stories. The fictitious and real life characters of his writing are central to the concerns of the work, it is their story which allows us to enter into the realm of the marginalized. By assigning the centrality to the marginalized characters, Ghosh also answers the dilemma of the postcolonial intelligentsia regarding the ability of the subaltern to speak. Here is a writer who belongs to a once colonized country, has received Western training and is a glob trotter, witnessing various issues of life of our postcolonial world and is not hesitant to speak or opine on subaltern issues. His own association with the group and practice of the discourse empowers him to entail it in his writings. Now the issue of whether an 'outsider' though from a colonized world but fairly placed in social hierarchy and associated with Western academia can be a representative of the subalterns is answered in a unique manner. He doesn't become the representative; he assumes the role of a narrator of a narrative which allows the representations of the subaltern group by the same group. His works strongly confirm to the notion that the subaltern can speak if given a proper chance and with an appropriate employment of the discourse into both fictional and non-fictional writings.

His first novel *The Circle of Reason* is peopled with the characters drawn from the lower strata of the society. Lalpukar is a village near Calcutta where destiny takes orphaned Alu and the story of the novel is set into motion. Alu, Shombhu Debnath, Rakhal, Toru Debi, Rajan, Zindi-al-Aiffaha, Kulfi, Karthamma, Jeevanbhai Patel, Haji Fahmy, Zaghloul all these characters belong to the subaltern group and are involved in the work/profession that is not looked upon with respect in the society. It is interesting to see that Balaram practices Phrenology, a less respected branch of science. Through him, Ghosh brings in the discourse of Marxism and class struggle. He teaches subjects like weaving and principles of sanitation in his school. Except for the people from Bhudeb Roy's side, majority of the characters from the village are from the lower middle class or lower class. Alu's journey from village to Calcutta and from Calcutta to al-Ghazira introduces more characters with similar background. At al-Ghazira, Alu lives in the house of a former prostitute named Zindi who shelters all sorts of refugees even people with questionable past and professions. Alu's life here is an insight into lives of refugees in the Gulf. It is noteworthy that *The Circle of Reason* came into existence before the author's involvement with Subaltern Studies Group. However, it sets the writer's interest in the lives of people from marginalized class. With the advancement of his writings, many more such characters are introduced to the readers.

The Circle of Reason also sets the tone of the author's concerns about the issues of the lives of powerless. Alu's life is completely jeopardized because of Bhudeb Roy. As the novel progresses, he turns out to be a complete political bully. He invites Balaram to teach in the school but as the time passes, the rivalry between the two takes an ugly shape. Budheb Roy is powerful both economically and politically. This enables him to devastate Balaram's world. In the initial phase, he gets Balaram's fish pond poisoned, his sons try to molest Maya. The dispute takes an ugly shape when Balaram destroys his public rally; Bhudeb plots to kill the entire family. Thus, the powerful destroy the lives of people without power. Even after the death of entire family, Bhudeb is not satisfied and manages Jyoti Das to believe that Alu is the culprit of the murder of his own family. Alu is pushed into a life of a permanent refugee and forced to move from one place to another in order to escape imprisonment.

Thus, the first novel encompasses the concerns and characters that can be of an interest to subaltern studies. One of the major themes of the novel is the struggle of a not so heroic hero. The other characters are also drawn with grayish shades. They belong to the 'minority' class in one or the other way, not a part of the main stream of the society.

The second fiction *The Shadow Lines* is based more on the questions of nations, identity and borders. However, one character, namely Tridib, befits the category of the marginalized in a broader sense of the term. He belongs to the world of ideas. A hard core romantic, he belongs to a category which doesn't get chance to decide in the society. He is the one who thinks very differently and perceives the world in a different manner. The novelist's interest lies in listening to voices of the marginalized anonymous individual, a group of people whom history doesn't take any record of an unknown slave in *In an Antique Land*, a mysterious pair of tribal who intervene in the elitist scientific research by the colonizers in *The Calcutta Chromosome*, a poor fisherman in *The Hungry Tide* mirror the locus of the author's interest in subaltern individuals.

The stress is on the unpredictable nature of human existence that acts as a strong background in his writings through characters. They are simply unimportant individuals like Alu in *The Circle of Reason*, Bomma in *In an Antique Land*, Laakhan in *The Calcutta Chromosome*, Tridib and grandmother's poor relations in *The Shadow Lines* or Ilongo and Kishan Singh in *The Glass Palace*. They are voiceless nobodies. Ghosh purposefully brings them into stories and focuses on personal histories of such individuals. They are always on the fringe; they are always floating signifiers who have to fleet endlessly.

When he talks about an individuals' experience during historical events, the majority of the individuals are from the class which history tends to overlook. There are some characters who belong to the centre of the power group. The marginalized characters help us envisage life, events and issues from their point of view. *The Hungry Tide* is peopled with such characters. Fokir is a unique character that acts as a representative of all those unsung and unheard heroes of tide country. His life has been a struggle from early childhood, throughout the novel he emerges as a silent hero who is not much respected either in his society or by his wife.

Kusum in *The Hungry Tide* stands for such not so 'noteworthy' or 'historical' individuals who have a capacity to change the mindset of those who cross their lives. Nirmal is taken to Morichjhapi by Horen where he meets Kusum after years. He happens to see the entire movement of Morichjhapi through Kusum's eyes and finds the type of revolution he sought throughout his life. This revolution is from below which is being evinced by voiceless nobodies who want to be heard. Nirmal begins to identify himself with them. For him the cry of the refugees becomes a representative of all such subaltern communities without home. He says:

> How strange it was to hear this plaintive cry wafting across the water. It seemed at that moment, not to be a shout of defiance, but rather a question being addressed to the very heavens, not just for themselves, but on behalf of bewildered humankind. Who, indeed, are we? Where do we belong? (Ghosh 2004: 254)

Ghosh has extended the reach of Subaltern Studies Group by giving agency to the subaltern in *The Calcutta Chromosome*. Commenting on this Tabish Khair says,

> In *The Calcutta Chromosome*, significantly, the human sacrifice is taken over and reinscribed within the subaltern's agency and the subaltern's (suggested) discourses. From that perspective, it becomes a form of discovery, of furthering life and of planned, purposive activity. It becomes in a way the exact opposite of what 'barbaric' and 'irrational' stand for—a planned means of personal improvement and collective well-being. (Khair 149-50)

The conspiracy is planned not with an intention of destruction. In fact, the conspiracy becomes a bridge that joins the scientific research and cult practices. Thus, here the subaltern agency stands as a mediator between practices of science and technology and the world of 'other knowledge system'. It is also an intriguing example of how binaries intervene in the evolution of each other and instead of becoming binary oppositions; they act as complementary for the growth. The occult practices of Mangala and her group seems quite opposite to the neat and scientific research for Malaria. But they direct the research by providing him information in bits and pieces leading Ross towards the final discovery. They conspicuously provide leads at times and at places that are predetermined in their scheme. Thus, the subaltern acts as the agency on which the established power builds up its discourse.

The theme of *The Calcutta Chromosome* is based on the research on the Malaria bug and its connection with Syphilis is a dauntless play of the centre and the margin. It is an innovative way of lending central position to the people in margins. Murgan, the central character is actually writing history of research on Malaria which is not the history as known. So here is a character who is practicing the theory posed by Subaltern Studies Group. Mangala and her cult remain in the margin, visible only in glimpses, rather as a mystery manipulating the entire research. Thus, here margin manages the centre. The entire play of this displacement of 'centrality-power' by 'margin-powerless' is so subtly designed as the marginalized have the real power and the centre is always under an illusion of having the control and power: the power of knowledge, power of authority, power of superiority provided by the fact of being the member of a race that ruled the so-called 'third world'.

Subaltern Studies Group tried to fill the gaps of history, which is written by elites, by recognizing, recovering, restructuring and identifying the stories of non-elite, subjugated and marginalized people. The fictions by Ghosh are based on such stories. The intention of penning down such events which are not noticed in official history behind many of his writings is hinted upon by Nirmal's purpose behind writing his journal. He notes, "How skilful the tide country is in silting over its past…perhaps I can make sure at least that what happened here leaves some trace, some hold upon the memory of the world" (Ghosh 2004: 69).

His work is woven with such unknown people and their unknown stories and hardly known places like Fustat, Lusibari, etc. The heavy hands of power wish them to be silenced forever but the very act of silencing them leads towards a way that voices their speech. They develop their own system that saves them from being removed. So Ghosh remarks, "full of these ghosts, these unseen presences whose murmurings could never quite be silenced no matter how loud you spoke" (Ghosh, 2004: 220).

His representation or practice of subaltern theory is not restricted to characters. The issues he addresses are also of marginalized category. The themes evoked in his works are in tune with the concerns of subaltern theory. As mentioned above, the struggle of people in Morichjhapi is a befitting example of the same.

Thus, the continuity of the subaltern agency and the presence of subaltern against the sprawling carpet of power that covers their presence coexist in the society. The continuity of subaltern agency and irremovable presence of subaltern people and places surviving against the drowning dominant power structures get reflected in the wide scope of the narratives in Ghosh.

In *The Glass Palace*, we come to know about the lives of servants, governesses and urchins after the downfall of the royal couple. *The Glass Palace* spans over three generations and three countries. Indian settlement in Burma is almost negligible in Indian literature. Somehow it has been overlooked by the historians too. Especially, the accounts of the people who made Burma their house during the years of British invasion on Burma, is almost invisible amongst the footprints noted in history. Burma has been in turmoil for various reasons for more than a century. It is strange to realize that public records in India hardly remember the upheavals that jolted this country which is geographically so much in proximity.

Amitav Ghosh's fathers' family lived in Burma for several generations. *The Glass Palace* is partially written because of his personal awareness and research of the mayhem in the country in the neighbourhood. He was inspired to record some of the historical events of the country due to realization of absence of records of Indian presence in Burma. Thus, the foundation of this fictional work is laid down on historical facts. Here again, Ghosh fictionalizes the event of great exodus from Burma, an event which remain silent in public domain. It also shows the extent to which Indians were mentally colonized by the Britishers. He has told a reporter,

> ...(Long March) It's not written about at all.... It's strange—there were over half a million people on the Long March, over 400,000 of them Indian, and there is such a silence about it.... There was no need for the Indians in Burma to flee when the Japanese approached—many Indians did stay back. It makes you realize the degree to which Indians felt themselves to be the sheep of the British; the delusions that governed their lives. (*Outlook Interview*)

This novel opens up with the story of an orphan boy, Rajkumar who is brought to Mo Chao's stall in the capital of Burma as the ship he used to work was not able to move forward. Again Mo Chao is a character that is lower in social and economical rank. She runs a small food stall. Rajkumar gets a shelter in her stall with a condition to work for her. Mo Chao's life is ruthlessly shattered by imminent devastation caused by British invasion. She leaves the place and is lost from the pages of story like millions who are erased from the memory of human society. Like those irretrievable figures, she too, is ruined and drowned in the tides of social and political turmoil. Fascinated Rajkumar joins the group of people who ransack through the royal palace. During this ruckus, he happens to see Dolly, a young attendant of the queen, a central figure of the novel again drawn from the lower social group. Dolly is transferred to Ratnagiri along with the crest fallen royal family, Rajkumar on the other hand, works hard and becomes a successful, rich businessman by indulging in profit-making exploitations of natural resources and people of Burma. Life of the royal family and Dolly pass through myriad events with the course of time. The king and queen scale down in social hierarchy and rank as their lives are 'looked after' by the British Rule. Here the king ponders on the force and nature of power of British Empire that was changing fates of thousands across the subcontinent.

> What vast, what incomprensible power, to move people in such numbers from one place to another—emperors, kings, farmers, dockworkers, soldiers, coolies, policemen. Why? Why this furious movement—people taken from one place to another, to pull rickshaws, to sit blind in exile? (Ghosh 2000: 43-44)

Again, an example of how people in centre can shift to the margins. Thus, ironically, the royal family is reduced to the status of subalterns. However, the queen in her true spirit, defies the reduced status in as many ways as possible. She allows villagers to live near the house during the time of plague. From this point onwards, the novel gets further populated with more characters from the lower ranks of society. The time span of the novel makes space for the monstrous manifestations of exploitation from the time of colonialism to the period of neocolonialism. Ghosh points out the fact that Indians were also responsible for such exploitation of people and place. Through the voice of Uma, Ghosh lashes out against all Indians who participated in the process of exploitation due to the manipulative Victorian Policy. She tells Rajkumar,

> It's people like you who're responsible for this tragedy. Did you ever think of consequences when you were transporting people here? What you and your kind have done is far worse than the worst deeds of the Europeans. (Ghosh, 2000: 214)

Another unexplored aspect of Indian history also finds a voice in this novel. The history of Indian Army under British Rule is completely oversighted in the discussion of the colonial past in terms of what it meant for those who had joined British Army. Through the characters like Hardayal, Kishan Singh and Arjun Ghosh brings in the plight of Indian soldiers serving Britain and on the war front in Burma. Like *The Calcutta Chromosome*, here too it is the subaltern—Kishan Singh who makes Arjun realize few realities in life. Thus, again it is the powerless who own power in terms of knowledge. This time the knowledge is of one's own identity and worth in the large world. Interestingly being a batman, Kishan Singh is actually lower in rank to Arjun and thus an easily identifiable subaltern. Again as an answer to Gayatri Spivak's question it is Arjun whose class and agency changes in accordance with time and space. Arjun derives a more comprehensive understanding from Kishan Singh about the insignificance of individuals like him in the larger canvass of historical and powerful forces. He realizes that it has always been a force of larger powers that had controlled his life. He starts reflecting upon his own life and asks,

> Was it possible—even hypothetically—that his life, his choices, had always been moulded by fears which he himself was unaware?... Then it would follow that he had never acted of his own volition; never had a moment of true self-consciousness. Everything he had ever assumed about himself was a lie, an illusion. And if this were so, how was he to find himself now? (Ghosh 2000: 372)

The strength of British power and its penetration into various classes in Indian society is aptly captured in various episodes of *Sea of Poppies*. If soldiers like Arjun in *The Glass Palace* were used to capture more territories, people like Hawaldar in *Sea of Poppies* on the ship were given utmost liberty to harass and torture their own people in the name of tradition. The episode of Kalua being beaten monstrously on the ship by the Indians for getting married and spoiling a high caste woman subverts the British claim of being the harbinger of social reformation in India. Thus again the novel speaks against the colonialism and debunks the discourse of the colonizers as the social reformer of Indian society. This also speaks for the unwritten stories of doubly subaltern people—people who were lower in rank within a colonized society.

The experiences at the small village in *In an Antique Land* entails other issues that extends the issue of subaltern. It narrates the history of people and place where in the subaltern issues are located and reconstructed on the basis of the 'traces' available in libraries. The innovation in this work has earned well deserved responses from the critics. For example, John Hawley remarks, "*In an Antique Land* is an unusually constructed book that deals with themes of historical and cultural displacement, alienation something we might call 'subaltern cosmopolitanism'" (Hawley 89).

In an Antique Land traces subaltern character from medieval time. The attempt to retrieve an individual's life leads to retrieval of Indo-African trade system and society in Mangalore during 15th century. As a young researcher from Oxford, Ghosh seems to have experienced the paradigms of how the West appropriated the history and society of the Third World countries. The strands of history are connected with the present in a manner that reflects the continuity of power politics and the resultant subaltern. Commenting upon this, Robert Dixon says,

> 'Bomma' is the subaltern consciousness whose recovery justifies Ghosh's allegorical reading of the destruction of a polyglot trading culture by Western influence. Unlike some contributors to Subaltern Studies, Ghosh develops a style of writing that is sufficiently nuanced and elusive to sustain the 'theoretical fiction' of a recovery of presence without actually falling back into essentialism. (Dixon 18)

Like *In an Antique Land*, the focus is on lives of individuals in *Dancing in Cambodia*. He meets people one by one to have an understanding of the implications of prevailing situation at micro level. He begins a string of individual accounts with the story of Moyaka who had lost her father, two brothers and seven other family members during Pot Pol's regime. This is a point when Ghosh makes his general observations on the revolution. He describes a society full of individuals who are trying to build up a hope for themselves from the ruins and rubbles created by Pol Pot's regime. These accounts also stand for the fact that how the presence of UNTAC forces in Cambodia was not helpful to people. Cambodians had become doubly threatened because of the political developments.

Here also the subalterns speak for themselves. They voice their stories of suffering. It is a novel way of representing subaltern voices. The psyche and soul of people at large are fractured but they exhibit a resilient spirit. Everywhere there are hopes and efforts for resurrection out of ruins. This is a moving account of actual survivors in Cambodia who are trying to rebuild their lives "like rag pickers, piecing their families, their roofs together from whatever little that was left" (Ghosh 1998: 19).

Each story is an account of silenced suffering and struggle. The situation in Cambodia was of chaos everywhere, the storm had not settled yet. The survivors of Khemer Rouge carnage were living continuously under the threat of government officials also. Ironically, the harbingers of law, the police and soldiers were the biggest threat to people's safety and security. Ghosh summarizes this situation in following words: "The government's underpaid (often unpaid) soldiers and policemen were increasingly prone to banditry and bouts of inexplicable violence" (Ghosh 1998: 8).

He narrates a story of the victims whom he met at hospital. These women and children who had suffered fatal injuries as some soldiers detonated a fragmentation of mine. The reason for this gruesome act was that the women did not give all the money they had earned that day. They had already given some of the earnings of that day but these greedy 'soldiers' wanted all and when their greed was not satisfied the ammunition meant to protect civilians was used to kill the citizens. Ghosh himself encountered similar life threatening experience during one of his visits to individuals. This was a situation of uncertainty and insecurity. People wanted to secure themselves by all fair and unfair means as nobody was sure of future, this was propelled further by the announcement of UN sponsored election. So all those who had some power including ministers, bureaucrats, policemen and soldiers, were exercising it to loot as much as possible. This is well captured in these words: "Paradoxically, at precisely the moment when the world had ordained peace and democracy for Cambodia, uncertainty had reached its peak within the country" (Ghosh 1998: 11).

The stories of people in *Stories in Stones* also depict the intensity of torture on middle class during Pol Pot's regime and how some people lived it through. Kong Sarith's memories of the camp is one of them. He was studying in second year when Khemer Rouge entered Phnom Penh. He was taken to a labour camp few miles away from Sisophon. He realized quickly that if he revealed his identity to the soldiers, they would surely kill him. So he made up a story about his background and introduced himself as a waiter in a roadside eating place. For which he was interrogated also and made to wake up at 2.30 in the morning to wash dishes besides the regular draining work on rice fields during the day. He was married forcefully with a woman in the camp. Their marriage survived for their shared suffering. They were released on January 4, 1979. While marching their way towards Phnom Penh to find his family, he met many like him who were educated and had professional trainings also but had to hide their real identities to remain alive.

Like in fiction, his characters are drawn from subaltern class in non-fiction too. He focuses on such individuals. The purpose of subaltern studies is well served by making these people have their own voice. The conflict between the decision-making power centres and the people whose lives are decided by such power centres is not a matter of past. In fact, it is a universal conflict, so Ghosh furthers the practices of subaltern studies of deriving the 'other voices' from the past, by picking up subaltern real life characters from present.

He begins his essay on Burma by his memory of the stories of his relatives who had been in Burma and had witnessed the glory and downfall of the country. Ghosh always found these stories very intriguing. It was in 1962 when General Ne Win came to power and Burma began to be distant, secluded place. He says that immediately after taking charge of the country, "He slammed the shutters and switched off the lights: Burma became the dark house of the neighbourhood, huddled behind an impenetrable, overgrown fence. It was to remain shuttered for a almost three decades" (Ghosh 1998: 65).

Amitav Ghosh visited this "invisible" (Ghosh 1998: 66) country in 1995 and 1996. In his essay *At Large in Burma*, he records the voices of Kerenni refugees along with the voice of Suu Kyi on nationalism, national identity. He tries to capture the suffocating environment of Burma under military rule. The

Military rule had tried to silence the voice of people through enforcement of strict laws that intervened in even their family lives. He says,

> Every household in Burma must register its members with local authority; no one may spend the night at another household without obtaining permission from the local ward chairman. (Ghosh 1998: 78)

The author also mentions the fact of having visited a woman who had to stand in queue for obtaining weekly permission to stay at her husband's apartment even after three years of their marriage. The circumstances in Burma were bleak and the country was getting disintegrated due to various forces. Aung San had tried to build trust amongst four minorities—the Karen, the Rakhine, the Shan and the Mon and kindled a hope of union during 1940s but it all ended with his murder. His legacy was being carried forward by his daughter Suu Kyi. His visits to her gate side meetings reveal the complexity of the issue of the political commotion in Burma, the heavy handed grip of military rule that tried to silence the voices of democracy.

His detailed narration of the meetings and explorations in the Karenni's refugee camps give an overview of the life, struggle and perception of Karenni group. After spending days with them and people like Sonny and Mr. Htoo, he concludes,

> An insurgency, I was beginning to realize, is not just an army and a gathering of camp-followers. It is simultaneously a cause, an archive, an economy: an institution which provides for itself and develops a life that it will not cheaply relinquish. (Ghosh 1998: 98)

Thus, he makes the reader realize that the rebellions are often driven by ideologies; sometimes they come into existence as a reaction to resist suppression. Thus, it is again subaltern studies' way of looking at the other side of the insurgency. Ghosh visited the Karenni dwellings, an embodimentof the destructive effect of World War II. He views it as an enforced adaptation to nomadic life for more than six thousand people who are left stranded between Burma and Thailand. He describes the plight of Karennis in these camps. After talking to Sonny about various implications of possible political policies that can solve the problem, Ghosh thinks about "What it meant to live in a circumstance in which the jungle seemed to be the best of all available options" (Ghosh 1998: 106).

He also gives an example of a young man named Zin Myin to show how the appointees of SLORC turned out as rebels and escaped the military services. All these examples open up the complexities of the process of power politics and subjugation, the continuous flux in which the marginalized live.It also describes how people are pushed from one margin to other without any improvement in their plight. It also reflects that human predicament is not necessarily inscribed by fate, more often it is engineered by societal, political and institutional designs. His works capture arbitrariness of hierarchies set by binaries.

The essays in *The Imam and Indian* is a collection of the author's perception and interpretation of various subjects. Here also we have a range of characters who belong to marginalized groups. The Tibetan monk, the slave, Nabeel are representatives of subaltern groups. They are not heroic from the traditional point of view. History is not so much penned down for such people who fight their individual battles during larger turmoils.

The first part of *Ibis* trilogy, *Sea of Poppies* introduces us to a ship full of people who belong to the marginalized group. Interestingly, here we have a king who in other situation is a centre of power and society as a member of marginalized. His centrality has been pushed to the margins because of the newly established power structure; the British Empire. Deeti represents the subjugated woman in Indian society during 19th century. Married to an addicted and disabled man and raped by brother-in-law, she works hard to run her house and rear her daughter. After the death of her husband, she decides to become sati as she knows the lecherous designs of her brother-in-law. She has to part with her life if she has to save herself from lewd surroundings. This decision gives us an insight into the sati system also. Thousands of females with self-respect would have chosen death in order to guard their integrity. Luckily, Kalua saves her from this forced suicide. Both of them have to run away as this was an unpardonable act in their society. They have to move from one place to another in search of hiding as their lives are under threat and the clutches of caste system are both ruthless and far-reaching. Thus, finally their only rescue is escape from the country. They lend on *Ibis* in order to escape death. Thus, her story entails the questions on sati system, widow remarriage and safety of a woman within a family. These are the issues of Indian females who are already known as doubly marginalized class.

Themes are also drawn that dwell into the worlds of these marginalized people. Alu's journey to various places takes us to issues of people who are socially and politically marginalized. Only towards the end of *Circle of Reason*, we are acquainted with the people of higher middle class. Balaram's political adventures and school also operate as a window to this world. *The Shadow Lines* also touches upon the issues of people in margin before and after independence. It also gives an insight into the lives of migrants and partition. The issues on cartography raised in this novel complicate the issue of political divisions against personal and geographical proximities. *The Glass Palace* revolves around the issues of people on the periphery, people who struggle hard to come to the fore lines of social structure through economic advancement. The novel begins with Rajkumar's loss of his mother and his journey to Burma. Thus, he is an outsider in the country which is soon to be colonized. With the course of time, Rajkumar accumulates wealth and scales up in social hierarchy. The issues of colonization and India's freedom movement are woven into the fabric of the novel through Sonali's character. The world war again brings in the downfall of the empire set by Rajkumar and the positions are changed once again. The novel ends again with an issue of suppressed voices embedded in Jaya's visit to Dinu. Dinu is a member of a group that operates under cover to resist political atrocities in Burma.

To sum up his depiction of the shades of the term subaltern, following points emerge: There is an investigation and suspicion of origin, an attempt to trace customs and identities back to some original location, a suspicion of fixed boundaries (here in physical, geographical sense) between nations and cultures, traditions and identities, an absorbing play of centre and margins, enmeshing of cultural identities, complexity of the very play and shifts of nucleus, a demonstration of the fact that the subaltern can speak for themselves can be spoken about either through making them speak their stories or by creating stories on and around them in his writings. Thus, his writings are a demonstration of connotations and manifestations of the term 'subaltern' in contemporary writings. Amitav Ghosh is an author who belongs to the generation of established Indian writers in English in West who have international exposure and have strong sense of belonging to the cultural and national moorings. They have an insider's experience of belonging to a lower rank—a citizen of a country with colonized past, even after admission to the terrains of intellectually terrains. For his accomplishment in delimiting the term, Tabish Khair raises a pertinent question that sums up extent of Amitav Ghosh's endeavour to raise the issues of subaltern. He says, "Though there has been a great debate on the question 'can subaltern speak?' the more important question is 'to what extent can the Subaltern Smash, Shriek and Shout?'" (Tabish Khair 143).

Thus, the question raised by Gayatri Spivak about the ability of a subaltern and speech finds an answer in Amitav Ghosh's oeuvre. The issue of subaltern in his works is to be studied in two manners: first the meaning of subaltern as an affected practice, kind of parallel practice that existed during colonial period but never taken note of, as meant by Subaltern Study Group and reflected in his works where the author talks about the alternative histories and practices of people. Secondly, subaltern as an approach that takes marginalized beyond the inability to speak and empowers them to represent the marginalized people and their issues.

4

Confluence of Ideology and Narrative Chaftsmanship

The foregoing chapters have shown Amitav Ghosh's involvement and the manner in which he addresses the issues of Subaltern Studies and History. Thus, a close study of Ghosh's works show a continuous tension amongst various ideologies prevalent in the society. *The Circle of Reason* shows clear influence of Marxism which became a dominant ideology amongst the youth of 60s and 70s in India. The echoes of the same are reflected in Balaram's speech on machines. He says,

> Man at the loom is the finest example of Mechanical man, a creature who makes his own world as no other can, with his mind. The machine is man's curse and his salutation, and no machine has created man as much as the loom. It has created not separate worlds but one, for it has never permitted the division of the world. The loom recognized no continents and no countries. It has tied the world together with its bloody ironies from the beginning of human time. (Ghosh 1988: 55)

Again *The Shadow Lines* shows multiplicity of ideologies that prevailed in the society during various periods in the twentieth century. The riots stand for the disastrous manifestation of religious ideologies taken to fanaticism. The scenes from the time of the world war show the clash of political ideologies that shook the world in the wake of the twentieth century. Thamma's memories of Indian Freedom Movement represent the upsurge of the nationalist ideology in colonized India. Similar incidents that exemplify the tension between dominant ideology, often of repressive nature and a counter system of belief that challenge the hegemony of the dominant ideology is captured in *The Glass Palace*, *The Hungry Tide* and *Sea of Poppies* with the help of imagination. Such clashes between hegemony and resurgent ideology have also resulted in violence, destruction, displacement and uncertainty in South Asia. Ghosh has tried to capture the acuteness of such realities in the Indian subcontinent through *Dancing in Cambodia and At Large in Burma*, *Countdown*, *The Imam and The Indian*. Besides creating situations and visiting places, Ghosh also presents individuals—real and fictitious—who are believers in ideologies that represent the dominant power structures and the conflicts arising out of the societal structure. As the ideologies that Ghosh sets forth to explore are directly or indirectly an offshoot of Marxism, it is relevant to discuss in brief the views of Marxist thinkers on 'Ideology'.

French rationalist philosopher Destutt de Tracy coined the term ideology. He referred to the term to mean "science of ideas" (ideo-logy). The formative power of literature is often associated with the productive role of ideology. The debate on the role and effectiveness of ideology in literature and in the society at a larger level came into focus with Marx. In *The German Ideology*, Marx opined that what made ideas into ideology was their connection with the conflictual nature of social and economic relationships which characterized the labour process. Engels criticized ideology as 'False Consciousnes'.[1] Marx conceived of ideology to be a question of the superficial or misleading way in which truth is asserted and not a question of logical or empirical falsity. Gramsci emphasized on the role of intellectuals in creating ideology. His views on ideology were aligned with his concept of hegemony. He said,

> The intellectuals the historically progressive class, in the last analysis, in the given conditions, exercise such a power of attraction that, in the last analysis, they end up by subjugating the intellectuals of the other social groups; they thereby create a system of solidarity between all the intellectuals, with bonds of a psychological nature (vanity,

> etc.) and often of a cast character (technical-juridical, corporate, etc.). (Gramsci 60)

Like Gramsci, French philosopher Louis Althusser also refuted the charge of being 'false consciousness' levelled against ideology. Through his argument in *Ideology and Ideological State Apparatuses*, he proves that ideology is not merely an illusory representation of reality: it is the means through which people live their relation to reality. He argued that ideology is not an expression of the relation between men and their conditions of existence but it expresses the way they live as well as the relation between them and their conditions of existence.[2] Mannheim, through his *Ideology and Utopia*, introduced a wider definition of ideology and redeemed the word by using the word perspective to avoid the pejorative moral connotation of ideology in his *Essays on the Sociology of Knowledge* (Mannheim 239).

It was Terry Eagleton who could release the term ideology from its negative image and established its much deserving graceful position in the literary world. In *Marxism and Literary Criticism*, he argues that the artist does not 'create' something from nothing, but 'produces' a work that is determined by historical and ideological conditions. He brought out and emphasized on the interdependent relationship between form and content and that of a writer and social commitment. Thus, while arguing against the myopic view of new criticism, he situated literature in the context of society and dominant societal forces and in relation with the undercurrents of contemporary world that determine theories. He exemplified the relationship between literary theories and the ideological conditions in which they arise. He said,

> The largely concealed structure of values which informs and underlies our factual statements is part of what is meant by 'ideology'. By 'ideology' I mean, roughly, the ways in which what we say and believe connects with the power-structure and power-relations.... I mean more particularly those modes of feeling, valuing, perceiving and believing which have some kind of relation to the maintenance and reproduction of social power. The fact that such beliefs are by no means merely private quirks may be illustrated by

> a literary example.... To speak of 'literature and ideology' as two separate phenomena which can be interrelated is, as I hope to have shown, in one sense quite unnecessary. Literature, in the meaning of the word we have inherited, is an ideology. It has the most intimate relations to questions of social power. (Eagleton 29)

Jameson took it even further and suggested that literature as a producer of ideology and not just mere a site to reflect ideology. In *The Political Unconscious*, Frederic Jameson asserts the function of literature in ideology production. He opines that narrative form is to be seen as an ideological act which has a function of inventing solutions which can be imaginary or formal for the complex and irresolvable social contradictions (Jameson 345). Clifford Greetz in his influential essay viewed ideology as 'cultural system'. Ideology in him is "most distinctively maps of problematic social reality and matrices for the creation of collective conscience" (Greetz 64).

Like ideology, literature also plays very eminent role in cultural system. Specially in Indian tradition, literature has been an expression of dominant ideology and knowledge system. Thus, the thought and emotion are generally in harmony in Indian literary system. In general also a writer never creates a story out of a vacuum. The societal realities and belief system play a vital role in the formation and worldview of an artist. Dominant ideologies of later half of the twentieth century were understood and experienced by Amitav Ghosh. It is his belief in ideologies that make his writings imbued in theories like Subaltern Studies and New Historicism. Moreover, Ghosh is very much conscious of the role of an author and his own stand on his role as an author. His views on society, language, culture, human relationship, nation and geographical boundaries all are painted with his beliefs. These ideologies also determine his choices as a craftsman of storytelling. In an interview, he expressed the same in the following words:

> For me the value of the novel, as a form, is that, it is able to incorporate element of every aspect of life-history, natural history, rhetoric, politics beliefs, region, family, love, sexuality. As I see, it is the novel is a meta form

> that transcends the boundaries that circumscribe other kinds of writing rendering meaningless the usual workday distinctions between historian, journalist, anthropologist etc. (Ghosh in an interview with Michelle Casewell)

In another interview, he said,

> A writer is also a citizen, not just of country but of the world. When I feel strongly about some issue, I think it's my duty to express my views as cogently and forcefully as possible. (Interview with John Hawley 11)

The above-mentioned views by Ghosh summarize his stand and inclusive and innovative engagement with narrative as a medium of expression and representation. As established by the discussions in the previous chapters, Amitav Ghosh is aware of the dynamic ideologies and dynamics of the issues of contemporary world. One important point that has to be kept in mind is, Ghosh's role is not just limited to a storyteller. Therefore, this chapter also takes up his narrative style in non-fiction too. It is appropriate to discuss narrative as a mode of representation in the world of prose in the twentieth century briefly before studying the narrative features prevalent in Ghosh's writings. The present book studies both his fiction and non-fiction writings from the perspective of issues, ideologies and craftsmanship. Therefore, it is necessary to discuss about some of the salient features of his narrative and craftsmanship as a storyteller.

> As we continue to think about the uses of narrative in human life, we are paying interesting attention to the political effects of narrative, seeing storytelling not only as a way of creating community but as a resource for dominating others, for expressing solidarity, for resistance and conflict; a resource that is, in continuing negotiation through which humans create language and society and self as they talk and act. We see narrative more and more as a way of constructing 'events' and giving them meaning, as we pick out bits of the stream of experience and give them boundaries and significance by labeling them. Like all talk and all action, narrative is socially and epistemologically constructive: through telling, we make ourselves and our experiential worlds. (Johnstone 645)

The term, Narratology, the science of narrative that studies the nature and act of representation to examine the underlying narrative structure, was born out of Tzvetan Todorov's *Poetics of Prose* in 1971. As explained by Erich Auerbach, the Western narrative was largely rooted in Hellenic and Hebraic traditions. Narratology as an independent science of narrative flourished in the later half of the twentieth century through the theories by Tzvetan Todorov, Roland Barthes, Vladimir Propp and Gerard Genette. Story and plot are the two aspects that are points of discussion, though with different nomenclature in these theories and criticism on narrative. Shklovsky used the term 'Fabula'—for chronological sequence of events and the term 'Sjuzet' for the way story is organized. Chatman uses the terms: 'Story' and 'Discourse'. He said, "the what of narrative I call is 'story' and the way I call it's 'discourse'" (Williams 31). Gerard Genette emphasized on 'histoire' (story), 'recit' (narrative) and 'narration' (narrating) as the basic aspects of narrative (Williams 29).

Besides the techniques, narrative, as a field of research for its functions, emerged as an interdisciplinary area in the twentieth century in the West. To mention few, Schriffin showed how different storytellers create individual identities, situating themselves in their families and in society through choices they make as they narrate. Kirschenblatt and Gimblett also established that since the works of earliest ethnographers of communication the functions of narrative and speech have occupied a central stage.

As we know story is the series of events that take place, plot is the sequencing of those events and narrative is the manner in which these events are represented. All texts carry a multiplicity of meaning or polysemy specially so due to the representative nature of narrative. What is important in the act of narrative is the representation of the world with a purpose; an attempt to represent the world in as close and comprehensive a fashion as possible, using mimetic modes in a controlled, authorial way which survives to be read and re-read, without ever finally being closed or exhausted. It is pertinent to discuss the types of representations here. Hall (1997) has identified three approaches in representation: Reflective, Intentional and Constructionist.

The reflective approach sees meaning in the person, object or event in the world as it is and reflects the same meaning. The intentional approach is the one in which the person who is representing exercises the control. Here the representation is made to mean what the producer wants it to mean. The constructionist approach allows the meaning to occur: here the meaning takes shape through the representational system. Neither the producer nor the thing being represented has control over meaning in this approach of representation. All three types can be traced in the works of Amitav Ghosh. The essays in *The Imam and the Indian* are a result of reflective and intentional narrative. *Countdown and Dancing in Cambodia* resemble constructionist representation. The narrative of *The Shadow Lines*, *The Calcutta Chromosome*, *Hungry Tide*, *Glass Palace*, *In an Antique Land* and *Sea of Poppies* reveal all three types of narrative. His narrative technique is a combination of synchronic and diachronic structure. The premise of the discussion on Ghosh's writing, to study his craftsmanship, is based on the definition of narrative by Paul Cobley in his book *Narrative*. He sees narrative as "a particular form of representation in implementing signs…necessarily bound up with sequence, space and time" (Cobley 3).

The most outstanding quality of Ghosh's writings is the absorbing play of space and time. He adroitly moves back and forth in time and space, while depicting life in both fiction and non-fiction. Regarding space as a part of narrative, Ghosh opines, "A novel…must always be set somewhere: it must have its setting, and within the evolution of the narrative this setting must, classically, play a part almost as important as those of characters themselves" (Ghosh, *The Imam* 294).

The setting in terms of space in all his works is one of the most experimented elements of his works. The movement of chief character from one place to another is a way in which his characters and story evolve. *The Circle of Reason* takes Alu from West Bengal to Kerala. Then he sets on a journey that takes him to Yemen, Egypt and Algeria. The narrator's spatial movement, from a flat in Gole Park to Southern Avenue on Garihat Road of Calcutta, in *The Shadow Lines* add realism to the representation. The novel has exact addresses like 14 Lymington Road in West Hampstead where Prices live; the old house where Grandmother had lived once is in Dhaka was 1/31 Jindabahar Lane. Tridib acquaints the narrator with so many unknown places. This adds to the realistic locations of places. As for the imaginary places, the real places are described by Tridib in such a detailed manner that the narrator as a child is able to visit them in his imagination. Like the narrator, a reader is also required to broaden the limits of his/her mind to travel through the time and places Ghosh captures in his works.

The Shadow Lines questions the idea of nationhood and borders that divide countries. As Meenakshi Mukherjee has explained it through the metaphor of maps and mirrors, the novel discusses two aspects of looking at spaces: one as given politically or as that exists in the world and second in which one replicates the space in one's own imagination. Ghosh's engagement with spaces is drawn on these two perceptions in his other works also. One's own notion of space and the way spaces are distributed in real life are continuously juxtaposed. This is a repetitive element of his conceptual occupation in all his writings. Meenakshi Mukherjee's observation on *The Shadow Lines*, as mentioned below, can be extended to all his writings: "Time in *The Shadow Lines* can be illusory and concrete at the same time, and likewise space can be fluid even when held solidly within the concrete scaffolding of a house or confined within the firm outlines etched as a national boundaries on a map" (Mukherjee 261).

The treatment of space as a tool for narrative is also experimented with. Spaces are of two kinds:

(1) Physical/Geographical space

(2) Mental/Psychological/Emotional space.

Ghosh shows an extraordinary overlapping between the two categories. Characters from various backgrounds make such an overlapping possible.[1] In his novels, characters from different origins share deep emotional bonding than characters of the same family, caste or nation. Love across borders is a major theme in his fictions. It begins with May—Tridib in—

The Shadow Lines—and continues in *The Glass Palace* with Dolly—Rajkumar and Dinu—Alice, to *Hungry Tide* through Piyali-Fokir and also surfaces in *Sea of Poppies* in the growing relationship of Paulette and Zachary. This also subverts the paradigms of East vs. the West and challenges the arbitrariness of the way borders are drawn. This contention for border has been a preoccupation with him in all his works. In an Interview Ghosh said,

> What interested me first about borders was their arbitrariness, their contractedness—the ways in which they are 'naturalised' by modern political myth making. I think this interest arose because of some kind of inborn distrust of anything that appears to be 'given' or 'taken for granted'. This is why I distrust also the lines that people draw between fiction and non-fiction. I think these lines are drawn in order to manipulate our ways of thought: that is why they must be disregarded. (Hawley 9)

In fact, looking at his stance on the distinction of fiction and non-fiction, it is not a surprise to see all his fictions subverting many of the 'given' rules of novel writing.

As mentioned in the discussion on history, one of the key components of his narrative is a skilled use of various points of time within a story. The narrative of *In an Antique Land* is set in two time periods: the first is the twentieth century and second is the twelfth century. The present also has two phases: one is the time when he had lived in the village and the second is his visit to Egypt during the time of Gulf War; the past also stands as a middle point in past from which the author keeps moving to farther past and to recent past. The concept of time is exercised in an amazing manner in *The Calcutta Chromosome*. A reader is required to remain continuously conscious of the fact that the novel continuously seems to meander among three time phases: (1) The time when research on malaria was being carried out by Victorian Scientists, especially by people like Ronald Ross in India, (2) Murgun's pursuit of his own research on research on malaria and (3) Antar's present search on Murgun and events of his own life. All these events unfold themselves in an unpredictable and completely non-linear manner. Here it is expected of the reader to keep a track of each time phase and event from that phase to be related with when the next event from the same time phase takes place. His mastery over all phases and control over the plot and narrative is exemplified in the end of novel where all lose threads which seem to exist in parallel manner throughout the novel get rolled into one pin.

This effort of representing these stark realities is not deprived of literary achievements. His language becomes poetic and the realist representation gets an added dimension in his narration of real places in fiction as well as non-fiction. For example, he describes the first glimpses of Mount K2 in *Countdown* in following words:

> The landscape was of a lunar desolation, with electric-blue skies and a blinding sun Great sheets of glaciated rock rose sheer out of narrow valleys: their colours were unearthly pinks and mauves of planetary rings and stellar moons. The mountains rose to sharp, pyramidical points, their ridges, honed to fine, knife like edges. Their slopes were covered with pulverized rocks, though they had been rained upon by torrents of gravel. Along the valley floors, beside ribbon like streams, there were trees with whispering leaves and silver bark. On an occasional sandbank, dwarfed by the vastness of the landscape, there were tidy little monasteries and villas, surrounded by fantailed green terraces. (Ghosh 1999: 37)

Shifting terrains is again an interesting aspect in his works. The representation of spaces in initial fictions like *The Shadow Lines*, *The Circle of Reason* and *The Calcutta Chromosome* resemble the narrative techniques that were introduced by Salman Rushdie. Yet these novels reveal original innovations in the way Ghosh imbues the story with his ideology and the innovation of the use of spaces in the narrative.

The locale in *The Calcutta Chromosome* shifts in the same manner as we shift to various windows in computer. It jumps from the streets of Calcutta to Antar's house in U.S. and suddenly goes to the secluded, eerie railway station of Renupur. *The Glass Palace* also encompasses borders of Burma, Mandalay, India and America within its scope of stories of individuals. *Hungry Tide* is set in the Sundarbans and Lusibari and as with tide, we flaw to the waters of Irrawaddy also. The narrative also takes us to Piyali's parent's house in America. *Sea of Poppies* too, is a story of shifting locale. The story begins in a remote village of Bihar. The characters who are to board the ship are drawn from various places. As the journey begins, the ship is sailing in the Indian Ocean and the first part ends with ship still moving towards final destination but some 'jahajbhais' escaping from it near the shores of Andaman Nicobar Islands so we are promised with new regions and new flaws in the next part of the trilogy. This journey seems to be from many places to many places. Thus, journey is one of the tools through which he makes swift shifts of locale in the stories. Another aspect worth mentioning about these shifts in time and space is also a practice derived on the basis of new historicism. Instead of a totality, new history is being looked at as a shifting and contradictory representation of numerous histories. This allows the multiplicity and seemingly contradictory social practices to surface which remain covered in narratives of historical events.

As mentioned by Mark Currie in his *Postmodern Narrative Theory*, it is argued that narrative linearity and certain ideological functions of narrative act as narrative exclusions. A sign, an origin or a narrative episode can bear the traces of its syntagmatic relations and bears the traces of past and future parts of the discourse to which it belongs. Currie says, "The consequence for a socio-narratology is that narratives are not interventions of the mind but political and ideological practices as much a part of the material texture" (Currie 90).

Amitav Ghosh uses similar kind of a material texture for his narrative. Whether he meets people in non-fiction or describes events in fiction, the unspoken or unrecorded facts are entailed. It definitely bears the traces of past and future parts of the fact; though sometimes he does reveal these related facts of the discourse, often the reader is given hints about the interconnectedness of the events that are narrated and events which were marginalized. A complex structure of space and time resembling bits and pieces of jigsaw puzzle is deftly organized in an apparently simple narrative of his works.

Hungry Tide, *Dancing in Cambodia* and *At Large in Burma* are no exception in terms of this non-linear structure and overlapping of present and past. *Sea of Poppies* has quite a linear structure in terms of time when compared to other works by the author. But here also he tries to jump over time by giving hints of future events. Indicators/hints of future events are spread across the first part, for example, while talking about Zachary for the first time, he says, "as a child, strangers were apt to say that a pair of twinklers like his could be sold for diamonds to a duchess (later when it comes time for him to be included in Deeti's shrine, much would be made of the brilliance of his gazes)" (Ghosh 2008: 10).

In fact, the first part of this *Ibis* trilogy is filled with such indicative events that hint for the future events. The author creates situations and make characters promise few things which we as readers assume as a hint of potential future of these jahajbhais. *The Sea of Poppies* show how the turn of fortunes and cruelty of fate and society forced these characters to take up the journey which gradually leads to a brotherhood of shared pain.

Pain perpetrated through the infliction of violence and its memories play vital role in society. Ghosh's engagement with violence, manifestation of violence in the history and his own memories of such violent episodes are also an equally important aspect of his writings. *Dancing in Cambodia*, the essays in *The Imam and the Indian*, *Countdown* represent the real life issues of our world and author's opinions on the same. It also represents the ideology and his choices of his subject matters as a writer of here and now. Ghosh has altered his role, writing agenda and style after 1984, the riots in *The Shadow Lines* emerge from the author's memory of the riots in 1984. Suvir Kaul has also emphasized this aspect of narrative as representative of personal memories of a citizen in the following words:

> The pressure of this question—do you remember—generates the form of the novel: its partial answers, its

> digressions, its looping, non-linear, wide ranging narrative technique…for *The Shadow Lines* is an archeology of silences, a slow brushing away of some of the cobwebs of modern Indian memory, a repeated return to those absences and fissures that mark the sites of personal and national trauma. (Hawley 216)

Thus, individual memories and consciousness are given utmost importance in the delineation of an event. Bakhtin called all human utterances, including literary texts as social acts which are multiaccentual and available for divergent uses. He proposed a concept of narrative as a 'Dialogic' form which establishes characters as independent voices and independent consciousness that remain unmerged (Bakhtin, Trans. 1984). Ghosh's writings reveal this dialogic narrative. Even the non-fictions stand for overt heteroglossia. For example, the voices that we hear through the author in essays in *The Imam and the Indian*, *Countdown* and *Dancing of Cambodia* are reflections of autobiographical, biographical and critical utterances. Therefore, the switching over of time and space lends a beautiful quality of stories unfolding in its natural manner. As discussed in the chapter on 'History and Historicism', Ghosh places real events and real people in a world of fictive situations and fictitious characters. Similar method of problematising the distinction of fiction and non-fiction was adopted by American writers in 1980s. Based on reflections on one such writer, David Lodge identified four techniques of 'non-fiction' novel:

- Telling story through scenes rather than summary.
- Preferring dialogue to reported speech.
- Presenting the events from the point of view of participant rather than from some impersonal perspective.
- Incorporating the kind of details about people's appearance, clothes, possessions, body language, etc. which act as indices of class, character, status and social milieu in realistic novel. (Lodge 204)

The scenes from the lab of Ronald Ross in *The Calcutta Chromosome*, the riots in *The Shadow Lines*, the dialogue between *The Imam* and Ghosh in *In an Antique Land*, the scene of people ravaging through the palace at the time of the fall of the Burmese King in *The Glass Palace*, the dialogue between Nilima and Kanai in *The Hungry Tide*, the interviews of George Fernandez, army officers and villagers in *Countdown*, Arjun's reflections on the war in *The Glass Palace*, the description of place, people and their lifestyle in *The Circle of Reason* and *The Hungry Tide*; all these are few examples of the presence of the same techniques in Ghosh's works too. Thus, the practice that was being experimented and is being further explored by contemporary writers after the advent of modernism and postmodernism is an integral part of his works too. In an interview with John Hawley, Ghosh has also discussed how Ford Maddox Ford and Proust have influenced the narrative structure of his first two novels: *The Circle of Reason* and *The Shadow Lines* (Hawley 9). However, it is a resemblance that is visible in Ghosh's writings and cannot be labeled as imitation of these writers. This establishes the fact that evincing elements of changed forms of representations especially in novel writing during the second half of the twentieth century are also seen in Indian Writing in English through informed authors like Amitav Ghosh.

As a storyteller, Ghosh's chief interest is in the lives of individuals who continuously reinvent themselves. The stories both real and fictitious talk about how people constantly remake themselves along with constantly changing circumstances. Characters in his writings often resemble Chaucerian tradition of narration in which characters from various backgrounds set on a journey together. Each one is given a different story of his/her own. This results in two layers of stories: one is individual's own story before he/she embarked upon the journey and the second is the story of those individuals in a group and the story of their journey together. *Sea of Poppies* promises another layer of stories, i.e. an individual's story from where he/she falls out of common journey. He looks at the phenomena of migration as a process in which individuals change. Talking to Linda Grant during Tagore Memorial Lecture Series in Royal Society of Literature, he has mentioned that his chief interest lies in the phenomenon of how people continuously invent themselves during and after migration.

Moreover, travel and migration initiate a subtle process of extension of identity. Identities evolve and merge through cultural encounters and adaptation as a part of migration. The identities merge as the lines that delineate the difference are changing in contemporary world. Similarity of painful circumstances and shared history having been colonized bring people together. The author suddenly feels one or relates to the Imam in Egypt as he realizes the fact that both of them belong to countries that were colonized by Europeans. This lends a trait of fraternity among all the peoples of colonized countries.

Another peculiar characteristic of his works is the attempt to capture the issue of identity. There are two examples in *Dancing in Cambodia* which represent the issue of identity in postmodern world. One of the crew members deployed in Cambodia whom Ghosh meets in Cambodia, is from Ghosh's native, suddenly he finds a connection and affinity to this person. In Burma, he meets a boy born of Indian parents and thinks himself to Burmese. He has been treated as an outsider, *a kalla* all his life. It is revealed that he has become an active member of this guerrilla wars in order to reassure the people of Burma that he is one of them. Piyali's experience with the forest guard and Maje-Da also stands for the issues of identity and sense of belonging in postmodern world. Though an Indian, Piyali is perceived as a foreigner by these two whereas Piyali feels insecure with these two who are from the same country she originates from. Thus, experience of postmodern world is represented through an appropriate narrative that envelops various situations and encounters. Postmodern themes and situations are the key components. Issues of postmodern world are the chief concerns. His works also demonstrate the fact that postmodernism is not just style; it has become a way of life.

Again the issue of identity is dealt with in a novel manner in *Sea of Poppies* by camouflaging the real identity that leads to evolution of new identity, for example, timid and victimized Deeti becomes revered Bhabhi of all the fellow passengers on the ship. Another aspect involved is identity due to cross cultural movements and marriages. In *The Glass Palace* Dinu is born of Indo-Burmese parent. Queen who is thrown out of her kingdom asserts her identity by creating a 'parallel kingdom' in Ratnagiri and allowing her daughter to marry a man from low caste. Thus, identity here keeps shifting and is not limited to one's creed, caste or country. His works capture the evolutions and transformations of identities.

Ghosh's ideology and views on language is also a decisive aspect in his narrative. As with the other writers of 1980s, Ghosh uses English without any dilemma and employs the language with ease. He also experiments with the style and the manner novelists in English, especially from other languages employ in fiction writing. *Sea of Poppies* demonstrate the dizzying hybrid of slang words that were picked up by lascari speech which gradually made room in English language too. Set during the British Empire's opium trade with China and when India was an official colony of England, the novel is spread across northern India, Calcutta and the high seas in 1838, which establishes a link between different languages from India as well as other countries and the amalgamation of various words in English. Mrs. Burnham's English is sprinkled with Bhojpuri and other dialects of Hindi. The name 'pugly' given to Paulette stands fo the interpenetration of two Indian languages into English. The words like 'kubber', 'chull', 'dekkho logow', 'beech-o-beech', 'gudda', 'tumasher' are profusely used in Burnham household. This stands for the mutual exchange in languages propelled by the colonial encounter. The entire novel is replete with such mixture of languages. The intention behind such an effort of demonstrating a language in evolutionary mode is explained by the author in following words:

> the idea of fixity in language is so impossible and so unnecessary. Since childhood, we have always been told to use the correct English words, 'to speak properly' and we have developed a deep rooted anxiety about the language. But English used to be much richer than that, and the process of purification should be combated. (*Business Standard*)

His usage of such language is a result of his interest and research of language. Modern vocabulary has evolved as a result of cosmopolitan experience and various encounters. Ghosh traces the roots of some words and demonstrate it in this novel. Indian languages also got enriched in the process and thus the effect was mutual. He gives example of one or two examples that stands for his research on how a particular word entered in our language too. He says,

> At one point, 'banian' meant a sailor's tunic. It was only after the lascars cut off the sleeves of the garment that it acquired its modern-day meaning. Similarly, the word 'kamara' had a Portuguese root, and it were the lascars who first used it to refer to a ship's cabin. The influence they have had on our language is amazing, and we don't even know it. (*Business Standard*)

He doesn't provide any glossary for such words. Unlike other authors; he doesn't even use italics for such words. Another remarkable characteristic of his play with language is he puts the spellings of such words like 'dufter' (for office), 'tuncaw' (salary), 'kubber' (news) to reflect the European accent. So even the Indian reader also has to continuously keep on extrapolating between various manifestations of languages.

His stand on usage of italicized words from vernacular languages and rejection of the notion of translating the same for the convenience is elaborated in an interview in the following words:

> When I see Indian writers italicizing words, I'm amazed, because there are very few ordinary Hindi or Urdu or Bengali words that are not in the *Oxford English Dictionary*. In our age of globalization, there's this idea that English is becoming more expansive, but much the opposite is happening: in the 19th century, it was much more accepting of other influences, especially Asian influences. This is why I feel that if Asian writers like me are going to write in this language, then we must reclaim for it what it historically had. (*Business Standard*)

As an extension of the aspect of language as a cultural continuity, he brings in the aspect of oral tradition. In fact, John Skinner had appreciated Ghosh's narrative in *The Calcutta Chromosome* as oral performance on both aesthetic and ideological grounds (Skinner 8). Tabish Kher has also appreciated his way of narration as it restores the agency to marginalized. (Khair 145). The folk text on Bon Devi becomes a proof of documentation of oral tradition. Folklores remain alive within the people who cannot read or write. The shattered book in the novel stands for what happens to text, documentation that aims to keep the tradition alive. West is renowned for its tradition of documentation and Indian knowledge systems are blamed for its lack of documentation. But in India, it is the oral tradition that is meant for continuity of knowledge system. This debate on documentation is finely played here in the novel. Nirmal is surprised when he finds out that illiterate Fokir can recite the entire book. The contrast of two concepts is sharpened when an educated man takes it down and the one who is not exposed to written form recites it from his memory. The manuscripts of Geniza, the libraries Ghosh has visited, Piyali's GPS and recordings of her study, Nirmal's diary, the list of sources the author mentions in his works all stand for a continuity of knowledge, his documentation of his meetings with people and George Fernandez, people in Cambodia, Burma and Agha Shahad Ali speak for the author's belief in written knowledge system but at the same time he does not judge oral tradition as inferior. Language also encapsulates experiences. A continuous play of languages and use of vernacular language and dialects represent a realistic multicultural experience. Incorporation of myths within the fold of narration also makes the storytelling a comprehensive experience. So we are introduced to the story of Bondevi in *The Hungry Tide* and myth of Brahma of Siri folk epic in the "Slave of Ms H6".

Generally, what is indicated while something is being written, surface is story but behind it, there is history, politics and anthropology. This again showcases the experience of postmodernism wherein the lines are blurred and an individual is caught in multilayered situation. He also problematises factuality and probabilities. The dividing lines merge and ratio is played with. The issues are also from/of modern world. A world which is changing rapidly and the issues of identity, borders, castes, environment, relationship, science and technology all race up to occupy centre stage.

One interesting fact about the organization of the characters within novels is that each character is an individual and integral to the flow of the story. He also interweaves the story in a manner that ruptures any hierarchy of importance amongst characters. So if Tridib is an outstanding character in *The Shadow Lines*, the roles of narrator, May and grandmother are equally vital. The story of Murgan's explorations/adventures to probe the history of Malaria is woven with Antar, Lakkhan and Sonali. *The Glass Palace* can be called a story of Rajkumar and Dolly but then the story is equally about Queen Supayalat, Dinu, Nil Alice and Sonali. So there is always more than one character that occupies the centrality. This again is a highly postmodern way of life where the norms regarding hierarchy are changing. This distribution is not one against many or one with reference to many but the way in which one exists with many. This is precisely what happens in real life. The kind of fragmentation and collage that take place in contemporary world is revealed in many of the essays in *The Imam and the Indian*.

Again, it will be a mistake to say that only in postmodern world the individual is always juxtaposed, enmeshed or in conflict with others. It has been so since the time society as an institution came into existence. The postmodern element in the same is the blurring of dividing lines, the vagueness or lack of clarity of a role of an individual is something that conjures up one's psyche in postmodern world. The fragmentation and collage is also part of roles that individuals carry out in this period. Another way of looking at it can be his master stroke of debunking the system of hierarchy of roles and the centrality of 'the hero' in novel writing. For example, each character in *Sea of Poppies* is etched in a detailed manner. This sets the tone of the trilogy and also allows the author to eradicate the lines of central characters and marginal characters of his story. This shift is quite visible from his works *The Glass Palace* onwards.

His narrative challenges the centrality of hero and the notion of hero worship. This also allows the work to be 'dialogic' and fills it with heteroglossia.

The theme of relation between nature and human is an issue that has become a key issue in contemporary world. It is also remarkable to see that Ghosh indirectly gives a solution for this issue. *The Hungry Tide* depicts the traditional cultural belief of Bondevi and Dokhoi Raja. The favourable and supportive islands of the mangroves belong to Bondevi. After the fight between the protective goddess and demon, the goddess had forgiven the demon and allowed him to rule some of the islands. The ones who trespasses this boundary and Dokhoi Raja's kingdom has to pay heavily. Kusum's father gets killed when he goes to the island in the vicinity to get firewood. This island is thought to be part of Dokhoi's rule. The story stands for the fact how traditional and cultural wisdom is negotiated with favourable and unfavourable ecology. Kusum's father is a trespasser so pleadings to Bondevi also do not help, it is significant to see the meaning of the incident. The one who breaks the law of nature has to suffer. As a society develops and needs increase the human settlement spills over to hitherto unexplored areas. As long as nature and humans are in harmony the rate of loss on either side is negligible. But once the greed to control nature overtakes, the devastation begins. The people who have been living on these islands for years have observed/followed the dividing line. The refugees who try to settle down at Morichjhapi break the rule of the forest department and also disregard the traditional wisdom. The multifold complexity of this division and refugee settlement situates the novel in our time. The incident where the mob sets the tiger ablaze and Nilima's worry on the deaths by tiger highlight the acuteness of the problem of growing human population and nature's reaction to it.

The postmodern experience is multilayered. The political movements have changed the values and outlook towards life. The man-woman relationships in Ghosh's novel stand for this changing/changed notion of morality. The love scene between narrator and Marry in *The Shadow Lines*, the relationship between Sawant and Dolly, the memory of love scene between

Rajkumar and Uma in *The Glass Palace* represent the momentary relationship which lead to physical relationship as an outburst of emotions not necessarily love and sail on temporariness. These episodes capture the notion of love and sex in postmodern world. The silent love between Piyali and Fokir is an exception. Thus, Ghosh depicts the changing notion of love and sex in postmodern sense though most of the novels are situated in past. Postmodern experience is entailed in almost all the essays of Imam and Indian too. Piyali's character is representative of educated and independent woman of postmodern world. She is a catalogist, single and dwelling in man's world with ease. Born in India and brought up in America she has undergone a training that has erased the concepts of gender differences and the traditional ideas attached with womanhood. The incident where in Fokir offers her seclusion and privacy in his small boat gives an insight into the cultural underpinnings of two places: one that a person belongs to and the other which a person wants to explore. The gesture and Pyali's own reaction towards it, also gives an insight into the psychological experiences of the woman of our time and the meaning of modesty in contemporary world.

Amitav Ghosh, with his *The Glass Palace*, challenges critics to confuse narrative fiction with reality of nation by writing a historical novel, a narrative whose fiction gel easily into the empirically verifiable facts of the 'real' historical record. *The Glass Palace* unfolds over a hundred years of precolonial, colonial and postcolonial Burmese history as families are formed and individual characters experience loss and joy. Social organizations such as feudalism are destroyed and new ones formed in the guise of the colonial and postcolonial nation-state. *The Glass Palace* is a narrative that gravitates around the experiences of a multigenerational, diasporic Indian/Burmese characters during a historical period (the late 19th century to the end of the 20th) filled with battles won and lost over Burma's territories (the British then Japanese invasions, for example); it is a novel that reflects obliquely the great tectonic shifts that took place in changes of rule and national policy that affect the everyday of its characters' lives. As such, characters in *The Glass Palace*, its plot, and events can open its reader's eyes to acts of forced displacements and even genocides of peoples that took place historically; it re-visits grand historical events from different perspectives such as that of Gandhi's attempt at a social revolution seen from the angle of vision of the female character, Uma. It is a work of fiction, a novel whose complex organization deftly balances the referential (characters described in line with real people, places that have houses, mountains, rivers and so on, like real world locations, and historical events that can be recognized as such) with the imaginary to open its doors for readers to enter into its "possible worlds". Private and public narratives overlap, influence each other and merge remarkably in all his works. He encapsulates the pain of violence, displacement, sufferings due to war and national crisis. Such events of despair and bleak aspects of human life have found an expression in all his fiction as well as non-fictional works. His engagement with such aspects of human life that brings humans in tryst with destiny, nature or society reflects his interest in the unpleasant aspects of human existence. His writings are not meant for sheer pleasure or entertainment. Ghosh also ranks his writing as not as a joy ride in cultural reading. In an interview to one of the dailies he said, "May be my books should come with a blurb reading. This is not a happy romp in the playgrounds of culture" (*Indian Express*, 20 June 2011).

He does appreciate an individual's effort to cope up with life. It is of equal importance as the larger plans and schemes for national stature. An individual's small efforts to reconcile with life, is the actual point of change for the march towards peace. This is often neglected as he says,

> ...those tiny, cumulative efforts by which individuals and families reclaim their lives—a shutter repaired, a class taught, a palm—tree tended—and which are no longer noticeable once they are done since they sink into the order of normalcy, where they belong, and cease to be acts of affirmation and hope. (Ghosh 2002: 257)

Ghosh's novels also explore a vast field of communication, exploring both its possibilities and limits of language in human experiences. His characters seek to cross multiple barriers—the barriers of language, religion and social class, those between human beings and nature, between traditional and cosmopolitan, between urban and rural, between India and the wider world. The equation between global and local is articulated through the characters. This also makes way for intertextuality within his works. Chistopher Rollason has shown the element of intertextuality in *The Hungry Tide*. He proves the reference to Salman Rushdie's *Satanic Verses* and Herman Melville's *Moby-Dick*. He draws a parallel to Ghosh's story of Bon Bibi and Ayesha's episode in *Satanic Verses*. He also proves that the story of Bon Bibi takes the novel to a higher secularism by bringing in elements of Hinduism and Sufi beliefs—the two largest faiths within subcontinents. The reference to *Moby-Dick* is quite evident in the novel and it is also overtly mentioned in Piyali and Kanai's dialogues. Kanai tells Piyali "I thought you were going to lead me to my Moby Dick" (Ghosh *The Hungry Tide* 304).

The practice of referring to other characters and other works are fairly present in his other works as well. John Hawley has pointed out that Alu's metamorphosis and his weaving and talking to people reminds us of Kabir and Gandhi. This usage of myth also provides an element of identity, assertion of continuity of cultural heritage in colonized countries. Myths also voice the cultural wisdom and collective consciousness. Besides, the element of intertextuality such usages in the works situate Ghosh's narrative in the Indian narrative tradition. Moreover, it is just not a superficially added aspect to the narrative. The writings of Ghosh is deeply rooted in Indian cultural tradition which is of a melting pot of various myths and stories that have survived through ages. It is quite noteworthy that the collective wisdom in India is inseparable from myths and stories. So myths and stories have added to the Indian knowledge systems and vice versa. Keeping the tradition, magic realism is a chief element in knowledge building in *Calcutta Chromosome* also. Commenting upon the mythical allusions, eminent critic Samik Bandyopadhyay in his speech in a seminar said,

> In his latest phase, particularly in *The Hungry Tide* and the *Sea of Poppies*, Amitav Ghosh carries his narrative of colonialism to a mythical plane, with water as the historical element in colonial transactions assuming a

> healing, regenerative force, with its destructive power intact; in its violence, compelling people to rise above their prejudices and disconnections, and discover their capacity to struggle for survival. (Seminar 2011)

In this way, instead of a tunnel vision of narrator, Ghosh strives to have a hawk's eye view of the events. Ghosh's works provide scholastic and well-researched details of the subject in concern. Realism is reflected through societal depiction like issues of *Jat* and rituals which is an integral part of social life. Piyali gives an interesting historical account of study of Irrawaddy dolphins in *The Hungry Tide*, the details of anthrax in *The Glass Palace* all these details are derived and presented after a detailed research on the work. He has always explored the ways of knowing the world by bringing in the story or discussions on other systematic fields of study. If required, he explores the field himself to do the research required to incorporate minutest detail of such fields. His systematic approach of going back to archives to recreate the seemingly fictitious places and events are perceptible in his works too. For example, Deeti's visit to awe inspiring opium factory in *Sea of Poppies* is purely based on his archival research. He says: "In the British Library's archives, I found a very rare book, published in the 1860s. It was called Notes on an Opium Factory, written by superintendent of the Ghaziapur Factory as a tourist guide." He also admits having studied etchings and lithographs made by contemporary British artists. He adds,

> It's quite an imposing sight, you know, if you look at those rooms and the balls of opium in them—it must have been millions of rupees' worth. You won't believe how rationalized the industrial process was, and this is decades before Henry Ford. (*Business Standard*)

He also elaborates on nautical history of the 19th century with reference to *Sea of Poppies*,

> The Indian shipbuilding industry was absolutely on par with the Western industry, right up to the 1820s. In that era, a very large number of the Royal Navy's ships were built in Bombay and Calcutta. Then the British, through a series

> of financial measures and laws, succeeded in destroying Indian shipbuilding. And one of the terrible things that has happened in India is the way the shipping industry has been ignored. As late as the 1940s, it was possible to send something from Bombay to Madras through coastal shipping—it was easier and cheaper. (*Business Standard*)

Thus, he organizes his thematic material and ideology on the principles of craft of fiction which are language, narrative, technique and genre. Through his fiction and non-fiction, he accords meaning, purpose, relevance and integrity to past and present. Amitav Ghosh carefully organizes his narrative elements so as to both engage reader's creativity and simultaneously disengaging him from confusing invented worlds with the world that exists around us. His mastery over the challenges of craftsmanship is the sheer simplicity with which his narrative appeals to faculty of imagination and faculty of reason simultaneously. It permits to conclude that an author like Ghosh does not remain in an ivory tower. The guiding principle in his writings is to encapsulate the experiences of the past and his own time, the experience of pain, suffering, struggle of humanity through various times. He captures the essence of cosmopolitanism and revels in the world that exists in plurality with its multilingual, multicultural and complex web of human existence with its baggage of learning from the past and present. He synthesizes historical facts with creativity in a fine blend. There is no conflict between the facts and fiction in his works. His narrative is a combination of a serious scholar, details of an anthropologist and an innovative linguist and informed literary figure of contemporary world.

Notes

1. Engels wrote to Mehring, "Ideology is a process accomplished by the so-called thinker consciously; it is true, but with a false consciousness. The real motive forces impelling him remain unknown to him; otherwise it simply would not be an ideological process. Hence, he imagines false or seeming motive forces. Because it is a process of thought he derives its form as well as its content from pure thought, either his own or that of his predecessors" (quoted from McLellan).

2. Althusser's theory challenges the traditional Marxist model in which a society's base that is economic structure, material relationships of production and consumption shapes up the superstructure which includes state and social consciousness, including ideology. By giving autonomy to the superstructure, he empowered social practices and consciousness for producing social subjectivities. Thus, literature also gained a position to be productive and not just reflective of ideology.

5

Conclusion

As discussed in previous chapters, Ghosh's writings are remarkably imbued in his ideology. His participation in the world of literature is not just limited to the field of imagination but also in the process of generating meaningful and relevant literature. All his works since 1986 are embedded in his ideology on two major categories, namely (1) history and historicism and (2) subaltern. Both of these ideologies evolved and branched out in multiple interpretations and practices during the latter half of the twentieth century. As an author with ideology and cognizance, Ghosh has taken up history and subaltern as the central element to pen down his fiction and non-fiction.

All his stories are essentially about various points of history, how an individual existed, survived and sometimes got engulfed in the given scenario. Right from *The Circle of Reason* to *River of Smoke*, he consciously brings in his commitment to history and subaltern. A close study of his works reveal a systematic approach towards widening the narrower sights of history and making room for the people from subaltern class. He deliberately introduces the probable and possible characters in real life situations. He also creates fictitious situations around real life characters. This takes the readers to the hitherto uncharted alleys of history. Tridib's murder by the violent mob in *The Shadow Lines* stand for the loss of innocent life during riots that go to the peripheries of history. Similarly, Arjun and Ratan Singh in *The*

Glass Palace introduce us to the understated stories of Indians in British Army fighting wars in the subcontinent during the world war. On the other hand, he weaves a complete fiction around a verifiable fact and real life figure of Ronald Ross's research. Again, the downfall of the royal family of Burma initiates the family saga of *The Glass Palace*. This practice of fictionalizing history with a purpose of posing questions to the given history and also to provide the proof of parallel history that existed with the given history is a ubiquitous element of his writings.

He often juxtaposes the present and the past in order to explore these less travelled paths of history. One representative example of this practice in his works is the fact that the present condition of Cambodia is continuously contrasted with its glorious past. Again *In an Antique Land* traverses through various points of time from the past with a simultaneous trail on the present. This way of bringing in references from the past also situates an issue of present time in a broader context.

He also meets people and documents individual's history in non-fiction and documents it as a story in fiction. He also narrates history of places that speak for the other side of the Eurocentric or Imperialist version of history that claim discovery, preservation and conservation of culture and places. His essay on Angkor Wat is an apt example of refuting the myth of discovery and conservation of this ancient temple by the West. Another signature practice of his writing is the reconstruction of the past on the basis of documents. Thus, he builds up his writings on traces; he connects the dots of these traces together and carves out a story that would manifest the presence of parallel histories. In all his works, he invariably retrieves the other aspects of a given history. The latest work by him, is no exception to the way he gradually builds up the other aspects of history, in this *Ibis* trilogy, he builds up other histories during the Opium War from the traces available to us in terms of the records of ship industry that flourished near Bombay during that time, the factories that produced opium during British rule, the way bonded labourers and prisoners were shipped to other countries and using the history of the Opium War available in China.

In order to make the stories more relevant, realistic and engaging he weaves history both in synchronic and diachronic manner. His world of fictional works is situated in the pockets of history. He fictionalizes out of facts and known historical events. For doing so he relies on documents and archives and cultural memories. Using them as raw material, he projects some histories of the people whose lives and voices are never a part of the mainstream history.

Amitav Ghosh exudes a keen understanding of the political, sociological, historical and cultural moorings of his subject with an eye of an anthropologist focusing on history. Here is a thinker hailing from the discipline of anthropology and literature who revisits past through his literary critical skills and begins a chain of intertextual interpretations of those events from past. He focuses on ideological tensions, contradictions within the dominant power formations.

History is a discourse to understand ourselves better. With hindsight, we can see, construct and represent our future in a clearer manner. No present is exclusive or independent of the past. Various positions and debates on authenticity of history and historiography endeavour to enhance the perspectives of our present. It is not possible to study literature, as criticism of life without such a holistic vision. Various positions taken by Amitav Ghosh and innovative techniques through which he integrates history in literature land a deep insight into what lay in human development before now. Ghosh's awareness of various discourses, conscious commitment to his role as an author with social responsibility, his own experiences as an academician, journalist and an anthropologist shape out his writings as literary works with high seriousness. The reflections on history and representation of historical events in his works are remarkable for their precision and acuteness. His depiction of events from the past is derived from rigorous research and study of the events from various perspectives.

His use of the oral traditions and individual's own memories also add to the vividness of history. Stating this style in *The Hungry Tide,* a reader gets to know two versions of the growth of the place. There is a description of Sir Hamilton's dream of settlement and development of Sundarbans. This narrates the history of planned development of the place during the British Empire. In addition to it, the novel also tells us the folk tale of the origin and division of spaces within the region. This story of Bondevi represents the cultural wisdom of striking balance with the surrounding ecology through fear and reverence for the fierce and benign elements of nature. There is also an emphasis on collective memories and individual as a representative of the same phenomenon. Individual memories often render the other side of collective memories that allow space for the silenced voices to speak their stories. Often individuals' memory can bring in aspects of collective memory of a nation. Aspects Grandmother's memories of her youth in *The Shadow Lines* represent the fervor of nationalism during Indian freedom struggle. Such memories can also be memories of pain and suffering. Sudden outbursts of their stories by individual are delirious revisits of individual's pain and mute suffering as Cambodians. This makes the reader to enter and experience the torturous period of Pol Pot's brutal regime that changed history and fate of Cambodia. Memories of individuals as a part of history of a nation, is also one of his approach to acquaint and engage readers to the discourse of history.

He belongs to a group of writers who question the authenticity and power of history, historians and the validity of historiography. He deftly introduces the questions pertaining to the same in his writings. As a writer of fiction and non-fiction, he also seeks to come up with possible answers for the discourses he questions. Through innovation, he practices and strives to envisage a more comprehensive view of history. He crafts stories that represent parallel histories that could have existed simultaneously with the dominant history that is recorded for us. He also builds up on the fragments derived from the traces in the recorded history to construct lives of individuals and events that would have coexisted with the hegemonic history available to us.

As discussed in "History and Historicism in His Works", in the latter half of the twentieth century, it became an acknowledged fact that the element of fiction intrinsically seep into the factual representation of history. The traces are derived from various pieces of historical facts and information, the historical facts like British invasion in Burma, the proof of the trade of forest products in South East Asia, the use of elephants in timber trade, individual's experiences of the great exodus of Indians from Burma after the world war, the mention of women participating in Indian freedom struggle and the experiences of racial discrimination and riots in Burma all these traces are put together in *The Glass Palace* that spans over more than a century. This is a classic example of Ghosh's style of recreating tales on the basis of traces from the past. Here he also plays with the aspects of probabilities and factuality.

He does not limit himself to questioning of the discipline but goes beyond the given hegemony of history and introduces new practices in literature. This practice of placing intellectual discourses as an intrinsic element of his writings, enhance the reach and pleasure of literature. He delineates the knowledge aspect of literature without compromising on the pleasure aspect of the same. This also makes room for another aligned ideology of subaltern study and gives space to write subaltern history. As a writer Ghosh excellently puts the theories of these two ideologies into practice in all his writings.

His own consciousness of his responsibility as an author is revealed by his continuous engagement with the discourse on subaltern. As a practitioner of New Historicism and a member of Subaltern Studies Group, Ghosh focuses more on the parallel subaltern histories. He reconstructs, retrieves and resurrects some of the overlooked events and individuals and understands them. He also broadens the scope of the category by introducing subaltern issues and subaltern individuals from the present. Thus, he proves that subaltern is not a matter of past but continues to prevail in all societies during all the times, of course, in different manifestations. These concerns are intricate part of his writings. Various issues of subaltern class, the continuous suppression of the marginalized people from the ancient times till date, parallel practices that existed and survived and the people who represent the subaltern class all put together enhance the clarity of the kaleidoscopic view of subaltern as captured by Ghosh. He also highlights the fact that subaltern is a dynamic and live category that is receptive of the change.

A concern for subaltern issues is revealed in his writing. Subaltern characters play a vital role in fiction and they are introduced with utmost precision even in non-fictional works. This is an original contribution to the world of contemporary English writings which enable the subaltern to speak. Thus, a subaltern who theoretically remains in the powerless peripheries of society—in margins gets empowered and gets representation. By giving them central position in the writings, Ghosh conspicuously brings them to centre. Thus, he intervenes in the tension between power centers and the margins of society and shifts the positions of powerful centre and marginalized subaltern. With the representation of more powerful subaltern group that is in charge of the action *The Calcutta Chromosome*, he debunks the entire discourse of the rulers—centres as more powerful and the ruled—the marginalized—the subaltern as powerless. The life of an individual from subaltern strata; specially the life of the individual that go unnoticed during and after volatile period fascinates him and find apt representation in the world of his fiction. He also describes and meets people who are victims of power play in Cambodia, Burma, Pokharan, he explores the history of Geniza and the European intervention into Egyptian history and their perception and projection of Egypt to the world as well as the terrible experiences of people who witnessed the riots in India, Sri Lanka and Bangladesh. The turmoil, the situations that remain in continuous flux, the tension between power centers—all these aspects affect the people who are not playing any active role in these upheavals. He hits hard on the notion of the clear rift between the major and minor communities. He also endeavours to recuperate the silenced voices of those not represented in the historical record. Ghosh's ideological stand on the issue of subaltern is again dominant part of his writings. Based on subaltern themes, his writing is peopled with characters drawn from marginalized groups. In its essence, it is a stage for stories and events for people from suppressed segments of society. The question on a subaltern's capacity/ability to speak for him/her is worked out by the author by empowering the subaltern to speak for him/herself. Thus, they themselves are provided with the agency denied to them for centuries. In his works, the subalterns occupy the centre; therefore, there is a shift in the position of centre and margin. It also becomes evident from his work that Ghosh is not happy with the broad umbrella category of subaltern that show a tendency to lump all the marginalized people as underprivileged segment in all places and in all situations, another lopsided perception that portray marginalized as universally exploited class in all societies regardless of the differences that exist amongst various cultures and economy. Through his writings, he provides examples wherein a powerful person at one point of time in one society comes under subjugation at another point of time. A dominating member of one society becomes dominated in another society depending upon the changes in situation and circumstances. Thus, while enabling subalterns to speak for themselves he also avoids the blanket approach of many activists who tend to look at the situation and predicament of subalterns without taking into account the complexity and diversity of the category that is dynamic and vulnerable to major shifts in power and social positions. Thus, he brings in a broader approach and a larger perspective that take into account the fluidity of one's position in terms of power in a society.

There is a variety of manner through which he gets involved with subaltern. Besides the issues, he brings in characters that represent various ways in which the category of subaltern can be taken up in literature. For example, the character of slave stands for the standard practice of the Subaltern Studies Group of retrieving the other/parallel histories. He reconstructs the character of the slave from the medieval ages by an extensive archival research. Here, he puts the pieces of past together and tries to capture a slice of time of a society within which an individual lived and traveled. Again, the character of Fokir stands for the representation of stories of subalterns in fiction. He along with many other characters created by Ghosh stands for all those individuals who get engulfed in the sweeps of change and commotion. Interestingly, Nirmal is the character who records the struggle, and complexities of the subaltern group in *The Hungry Tide*. Thus, the history of the struggle of the subaltern group at Sundarbans is rendered by the fictitious character of Nirmal in this novel. Interestingly, Nirmal's practice of recording the subaltern is similar to Ghosh's own narration and documentation of lives of the people in Burma and Cambodia. Ghosh also meets people, stays with them and tries to give a voice to the unheard and unspoken stories of sufferings of individuals. These are the individuals who are fighting for their rights, individuals who have undergone agony of complete destruction of family and wealth. Thus, there is a continuous and conscious effort to represent individuals from subaltern along with a wider canvass of their circumstances in all his works.

Besides the trademark concerns pertaining to the issues of past and subaltern, some other relevant tribulations of our society from present and past remain the chief focus of his storytelling. Even the exploitation of natural resources, rampant in South Asia is captured in *The Glass Palace*. The areas with rich resources were all colonized by one or other; the issue of exploitation is projected in its multidimensional manifestation. It was not only the west that acted as colonizers and exploiters, many like Rajkumar would have been key figures in the history of exploitation in South Asia. Ilongo stands for the live evidences of the nasty extent to which the heavy hand of exploiters could reach. Rajkumar's illicit child speaks the untold story of the mute suffering of women who were exploited not only for wealth but for pleasure also. This is a question that occurs in *Sea of Poppies* also. Deeti's life in the village shows the vulnerability of females within the closed doors of family. Ghosh hits hard on the hypocrisy of social structures through the episodes of her life. A member of high caste family and a wife of a crippled soldier, she is raped by the family member as a part of conspiracy within the family. The helplessness reaches to extreme when she has to decide for a less monstrous option of becoming a sati to escape the gnawing letch of her brother-in-law. The members of caste are not or cannot be of any help to her in such matters. But they assume the role of harbingers of values and grace of society and to teach her a lesson once she gets married to her saviour from a lower caste. Ghosh exposes such dualities and complexities of power structures that control human life. This depiction of the clutches of power structures on individual's life finds a place in all his works. He traces such phenomenon right from the medieval times to twenty-first century. The struggle between the binaries of exploiter and exploited takes a central position in all his works. He tries to locate these within cultural, political and historical contexts of the respective society. Ghosh brings in the perennial issue of exploitation of female body as a site. History of power shows that the female body has always been under continuous threat and made vulnerable by the power centers. Marginalized females have been a victim of exploitation through the double-edged sword of labour and sex. Thus, right from the issue of female subjugation to exploitation of natural resources, from suppression of individuals to suppression of nation and ethnical violence all the issues that need some considerations, according to him, are brought to the surface of reality in its all-encompassing manifestation in his works.

Ghosh is predominantly occupied with 'complexity' as an aspect of our reality. Each of his works explores one or the other arena of complexity of existence. *The Circle of Reason* dwells in the complex world of an orphan along with the other emigrants. *The Shadow Lines* explores psychological complexity of an individual and of a nation during crisis. *In an Antique Land*, *The Glass Palace*, *The Hungry Tide* and *Sea of Poppies* explore the complex social, political and historical webs within human life struggle to survive during commotion. *The Calcutta Chromosome* focuses on the complexity of the given history of scientific research and the other aspects of the same history. *Countdown* talks about complexity of political actions, national defense and individual politicians like George Fernandez who exemplifies the evolution of political consciousness of the nation. Illustrative essays in *The Imam and the Indian* entail various convolutions of contemporary existence such as Tibetan predicament, hunger for power and wealth manifested through oil encounters in the Middle East, manipulation of awards in literature by developed nation to make entry in the market of the Third World countries, riots and violence in India, America, and Sri Lanka. Thus, the issues he opts for are complex in nature, therefore the medium of expression demands a skillful craftsmanship that combine issues and ideology in smooth assimilation. The contents are of serious nature so the stories are not meant just for recreation but the author succeeds in presenting them in a manner that doesn't read like a tedious ideological ground for debates on contemporary issues.

Ruminations on power, freedom, violence, pain and suffering dominate his fictional and non-fictional works. Non-fictional writings are a combination of enthusiasm of a researcher's rigour for facts, clear insight into history of an anthropologist, a social scientist's keen perceptions of contemporary issues and a novelist's perception and grasp on the personal lives of individuals. He is intensely interested in the methods of knowledge and in the ways of knowing the world. This is one of the central themes of his work. His training in anthropology and interest in science is all pervasive in the treatment of the issues he raises.

The mercantile world of the Indian ocean some centuries ago, division of labour in Egyptian villages, issues of refugees, human settlement and environment at Sundarbans, insurgency and turmoil in Burma, suffering of Cambodians before, during and after Pol Pot, Afeen Route from India to China, community relations during colonized period in India, geographical and psychological boundaries, nuclear test at Pokharan and its effects to the immediate surroundings and repercussions in Indian subcontinent, horrors of riots, biography of Agha Shahid Ali, autobiography of Babur, exploitation of natural resources during the colonial regime and currently in the name of imperialism all these as reflected in his works, demonstrate Amitav Ghosh's interest in diverse questions of contemporary world.

He is also perceptive of the theories that stand for intellectual imperialism. Amitav Ghosh hasn't fallen prey to the enticement of such categorization and alluring awards that stand for manipulation. Some of the categories are created to lump the historical and cultural differences together and to give a blanket identity which covers the actual essence of the culture and identity of the nation that the work of art belongs to. Subverting the power that such atrociously exclusive and homogenizing category based award exalt, Ghosh had requested to withdraw *The Glass Palace* from the list of nominations for Commonwealth Award in 2001, this stirred up a vortex of controversy but it effectively cleared the slightest of the doubts on his stand as a writer and regionalism. He has reiterated his views on such lopsided categories that manipulate and systematically outcaste the writers in other language than English.

He seems to have a more synthesizing approach towards variety where in the essence of a culture is not sacrificed to create harmony. Ghosh shows that the encounter of various nationals need not result in a conflict every time and humanity and noble emotions transgress the boundaries of nations. Ghosh exemplifies these exceptions in his works. *The Glass Palace* is based on such cross cultural relationships. Rajkumar is helped by a foreign national, the friendship of Uma and Dolly, relationship between Dinu and Alice and Princess and Sawant all stand for the unrestricted world of human emotions. People of different origins, cultures and nationality stand by one another in *The Circle of Reason* too. Same is the case with *The Hungry Tide* and *Sea of Poppies*. Jodu and Paulette share a special bond of siblings despite the cultural, social, economical and national difference between two of them. Thus, the cultural encounter can result in fine amalgamation of cultures. It is an example of how love, care and pain unite people during a period when cultural encounter was resulting in conflicts or subjugation of either of the two cultures. His works are excellent examples of fine assimilation of cultures and differences. They are the mirrors of truly cosmopolitan world which also suggest that there are certain universal human emotions like love, pain, suffering and compassion that cut across borders and bind people together. His unique achievement lies in the fact that he smoothly travels back and forth in time tracing history of events and negotiates it with the contemporary cosmopolitan world. In fact, he traces the presence of cosmopolitanism throughout the folds of history. He also points out the fact that the very differences which are creating disturbances in contemporary world have coexisted throughout the history and was also employed for the advancement of colonization also. These differences have also enriched the cultural varieties in India.

He builds the idea of nation and the idea of subcontinent from individual memories. This also comes close to Indian tradition of history through oral and personal narratives. He also talks about a non-eurocentric approach to anthropology and the idea of identity. This is also aligned with his idea of space that gets manifested through the deliberations on space in his works. He reiterates again and again on the randomness of political and geographical boundaries and various tools of dividing people. His works insist upon the fact that nation as a space with political boundary is not the same as it exists in an individual's mind. In order to substantiate this view further, he effortlessly plays with the linearity of time and space in his writings.

His achievement as a craftsman is also revealed through a fine assimilation of various debates and discourses. His ideology is manifested not only in the content but also in the structure. Ghosh writes with ease and with an awareness of the multidimensional nature of the issues he has espoused. Oscillating between the probable and the actual, Amitav Ghosh adds to the understanding of our worlds. The excellence of craftsmanship lies in the fact that all his writings are conceived, organized and narrated to represent his concerns. His writings epitomize the confluence of conscious delineation of ideology and narrative techniques.

One of the chief components of his works is the integration of topography with the flaw of narrative. Locale is always an integral element of all his stories. He describes all the physical features of the locales with utmost precision. The mountains, the rivers, the mangroves and the landscape are embedded in the stories and real life incidents in his works. Besides adding realism, this unique use of topography situates all his works in a specific local context. These local contexts represent the experiences and incidences that are universal. Topography in Ghosh also expedites the events like travel and resettlement. *The Glass Palace* highlights the harmonious living and coexistence and interdependence of man and nature and the usefulness of the topographical elements that sometimes lead to exploitation of a place. Ghosh also makes an effort to describe the adaptation and struggle for survival in the fierce topography in *Countdown* and *The Hungry Tide*. He deftly delineates the fact that it is a conducive topography that leads to settlement and human prosperity and it is human nature that leads to exploitation, displacements and disorder. Intricate relationship between the locale and the themes is another equally significant aspect of his works. Hence, the river, sea, land, landscapes, cities and villages in his works are so finely interlocked with the flow of the work that they are inseparable from his works.

One of the salient features of his writings is the continuous play with the aspect of time and space. *The Circle of Reason* relies more on shifting locales but with *The Shadow Lines* Ghosh added the element of sudden shift in time and space. All the works that have followed after these two novels reveal Ghosh's consistent mastery over the purposeful inconsistency of time and space in the narration.

Ghosh has introduced hitherto unexplored places and countries in Indian English Writing. He explores places and issues of places like Burma, Cambodia, Bangladesh, the Sundarbans, and Pokharan. His notion that distances are created more in mind and distances are independent of physical proximity or distances get obvious representation through the writings on such places. We, as Indians, perhaps know more about remote countries like America or England or Australia but we hardly know what is going on in countries like Cambodia or Burma which are relatively in the vicinity of India.

Another equally consistent technique in his work is the fine assimilation of various narrative techniques with the issues. Besides the element of time and space, selection of the characters, themes and use of language are hallmark of his writings. In the initial novels, Ghosh used some words from languages other than English with time these words have grown into sentences and dialogues. As a signature style, he never translates these words or gives glossary for the same. This again is representative of his perception of language. There are two aspects of such purposeful deviation from the general practice in Indian Writing in English. First and foremost reason is, language for him is a medium of expression and he doesn't use these non-English words to pepper his writings. It is natural for a person who lives in multilingual world like ours to use more than one language in communication. Such a use also adds to the realism in terms of language as a medium of communication. This also adds to the fact that in world like ours, writers in English cannot ignore the existence of other language. The second reason as often explained by Ghosh for the absence of glossary, is Ghosh's dissent with the regimental approach of writers in English. Ghosh has elaborated time and again on the inclusive and dynamic nature of English as a language that has enriched itself by absorbing words from other languages. Ghosh has also gradually built up the platform favourable to his love for words and language. He is interested in the evolution of languages and words and their fusion. *Sea of Poppies* show his gradual and firm approach towards regional languages and evolution of new languages.

His ideologies skillfully determine the people who occupy his world of words. There is a galaxy of characters drawn from history and from subaltern strata. As discussed in chapter on 'Kaleidoscopic View of the Subaltern' and 'Confluence of Ideology and Narrative Craftsmanship', there are similarities of background that all his characters share. They all are subaltern characters. *The Circle of Reason* portrayed a teacher with his humble background, a weaver, a mechanic, a tailor and a lady who rents her house to all these people. Alu, Zindi, Balaram are the first group of characters whom Ghosh introduced from the lower strata of the contemporary world. The character of the slave in *In an Antique Land* was created in a pursuit of retrieving life of an individual from lower social rank from the margins of the past. *The Calcutta Chromosome* introduced another type of subaltern group who manipulate the powerful silently. Here Mangala and Lakhan subvert the notion of overarching power that is perceived to rest with the higher strata in the society. Both of them represent the unconquerable spirit of people in lower ranks in the society whose knowledge and traditions survive the suppression. It brings out the continuity swarming against the ever-changing circumstances of a nation and its culture.

The fallen king of Burma, the Queen Supayalt and Dinu in *The Glass Palace* are the characters through which Ghosh brings in the lives of individuals who become marginalized due to the change in the circumstances. On the other hand, Rajkumar and Dolly are the characters whose origins are from subaltern strata who go across the ranks of society but are never settled in one rank for one or other reason. They are followed by the poor and dislodged characters like Kusum, Horen and Fokir from Sundarbans who are drawn together in *The Hungry Tide* to represent the lives of enduring people in the mangroves of West Bengal. Their struggle is double edged as they suffer due to poverty and the challenging ecosystem that they inhabit. Deeti, Kalua, Jodu, Paulette and Zachary in *The Sea of Poppies* too belong to the group of the marginalized. Even in non-fiction, Ghosh focuses on the individuals from subaltern category. Moyaka, Chean Chamy, the lecturer, the guerilla member of Burmese uprising are some of the people whom Ghosh meets in *Dancing in Cambodia* and *At Large in Burma*. They are the people who are systematically marginalized. They are pushed into subaltern category due to destructive and power hungry rulers of their country.

Women characters within this strata is again a unique and commendable feature of Ghosh's writings. Ghosh also confirms to the fact that a woman in the subaltern class is doubly marginalized in our male dominant society. He also captures the vivid colours of womanhood within the lower strata to represent the multifarious sufferings and responses to the suppression by the women in margins. Women in Ghosh suffer hardship and suppression but they are not mere objects of pity and sensuality either. On the contrary, women characters in Ghosh defy the oppressions and take charge of the situations. Kusum and Deeti are the portrayal of women who resist oppression despite the unfavourable conditions. These women suffer silently for sometime and show a great amount of tolerance too. But they also decide to stand for themselves. Instead of lamenting on their deplorable lives women in Ghosh's writings try to overcome the tyranny perpetrated by the man and society in general. Grandmother, Zindi, Queen Supayalat,

Uma, Mangala, Dolly, Piyali, Deeti, Kusum, Paulette, Aung San Sui Kyi, Moyaka, Nilima are the women who do not succumb to the overpowering subjugation. They are the gutsy, adventurous, firm and loving women who act during crises. They are the women who are in-charge of their own lives. They strive to work towards betterment of their families, community and sometimes their nations. The destructive forces of man are continuously balanced by the women characters in Ghosh's writings. This notion of woman's role as harbinger of peace and harmony is ubiquitously portrayed through one or more female characters in Ghosh's works. Ghosh's emphasis on the constructive role played by women in sheltering people and bringing back the normalcy during and after the riots that followed Indira Gandhi's assassination is an insight into Ghosh's view on the nurturing role played by women as a dedicated agent of resurrection of peace, welfare and advancement of the society that is under the clutches of violence, destruction and exploitation. Nevertheless, Ghosh also takes into fold the vicious elements of human nature that prevail in women too. Portrayal of women with negative qualities makes his world more human and rooted in reality.

Besides, these shared similarity of ideology-based conceptualization, Alu, Balaram, Fokir, Kanai, Murgan, Antar, Dinu, Neel, Rajkumar, Tridib, Imam, Kalua, Uma, Dolly, Queen Supayalat, Deeti, Alice, Paulette, Ila, May, Sonali, Grandmother —portray variety of human nature and psyche. Each character is a round character and stands for Ghosh's interest and insight into human mind and emotions. Each of the characters are etched as individual. We are acquainted with a diversified world inhabitated by idealists, eccentric, passionate, meek, intellectual, astute, stubborn, kind, assertive, firm, aggressive, feisty, docile and zealous individuals. A ubiquitous quality of his characters is the capability to hold onto life in adversity. Despite unfavourable circumstances, zest for life prevails. Same attribute is also seen in the portrayal of Aung San Sui Kyi, the Buddhist Monk at the Tibetan restaurant, the dancer of Cambodian royal troop, the leader of Karrennis. He is able to see the women making efforts to bring in normalcy after the riots in 1984 and the same ray of hope is perceived when he describes the dance of

Cambodians during his visit. Thus, his portrayal of characters or situations—real or imaginary is filled in with the optimism for life. The tension, the struggle, the suffering and the predicament portrayed in his writing is also balanced by a just representation of the resilient spirit of an individual and struggle of sustaining one's identity against all odds. Works by Ghosh exhibit the elements of both globalization and local issues. His works have a characteristic that is termed as 'glocal' in contemporary world. Some of the techniques in his writings are innate as an Indian story teller. He did resemble Rushdie in *The Circle* or *Reason* but gradually he has deviated from that cult and has evolved his own style and method. Unlike Rushdie, he doesn't get involved in India bashing or mockery. Unlike Naipaul he doesn't look at issues in India with a highbrow dissent. Ghosh has an added advantage of being a writer from India and abroad writing in English. Unlike contemporary writers in Diaspora, he belongs to India and is saved from the nostalgia of native and feeling of uprootedness as he still spends a part of his time in India while traveling and living in the rest of the world. An understanding of the Indian culture is predominantly present in the manner he takes up the issues of identity. He is quite aware of the fact that in Indian culture a man/woman always carries multiple identities so his works are saved from the much exploited issue of the 'pursuit of identity'. In fact, his works focus more on ceaseless evolution of identity.

He looks back at the past to derive meaning for the events that have affected our present and future. Some of the events from his own past have left undeletable prints on mind and therefore, are revisited in his works. The outrage and the sorrow of these events form his stories and essays and get related to the world. He connects the outcry of Agha Shahid Ali, a man from one of the most troubled parts of the world and the numbness prevailing in his poetry with the pain of his own and the numbness that humanity experienced by the new form of terrorism that emerged in 2001. The sense of loss perpetrated by the 9/11 attack become a point for him to rethink about the form and manifestation of violence that target civilians. His memories of the riots in India in the year 1984, the political suicides of modern world, the violence and loss of life in Burma, North-East India, Kashmir, Afghanistan and Central Asia make him trace the march of brutality and violence culminating into more gory forms across the globe. With the personal experience of horrors of the attack on World Trade Centre, Ghosh is pained to see the world moving towards a more incomprehensible violence which is not to achieve any specific end but with an agenda to fill the world with fear, anger and above all terror. With an awareness of the 'epistemic violence' that has torn apart the stories through which individuals link their lives to collective past and present. Despite the circumstances leading towards more unpredictable and 'utterly inscrutable' future, Ghosh still holds the hope for continuity of life and weaves stories mapping the past and unfathomable future to locate issues and ideologies of present world.

He also uses traveling as a metaphor for human condition, a world of disorder, a world on move, endless complexities of dwelling and displacement. The communities making, unmaking and remaking themselves represent dualities involved in human life; helplessness, predicament and conflicts on one hand and reunions, rehabilitations and rejuvenation on the other hand. He also draws in the aspects of cosmopolitanism through the blind alleys of history to our postmodern world. Interestingly, the narrative of these books entwines such qualities that make the journeys made by the characters in fiction and taken up by the author himself in non-fiction comprise various facets of human experiences. It penetrates the upper layer of basic information that travels generally provide. He pierces it and enters the subterranean layers of burning issues of the places, gives an insight into their problems and gives another perception to look at their problems. The poignancy of the problem, the unrest beneath the layer of so-called restoration and resettlements are brought to the surface. The intrinsic relationship between an individual and the society, community living, cultural aspects all get reflected and are reflected upon by the author.

His role creates a challenge that is twofold: he is an author who belongs to the intellectual world of discourses and debates that prevailed in the latter half of the twentieth century; secondly he is also aware of the reality of our lives in the sense of the gap that exists in our so-called progressive society. Moreover, he is also aware of the fact that he is writing for readers who belong to postmodern world of faster communication, are also aware of intellectual advancements and informed of their worlds. Ghosh turns this challenges into opportunity for developing his stories and characters that are created with a consciousness and awareness of the aware and well informed readers.

Contemporary world consists of plurality, multidisciplinary and multilingual experience. With the advent of discourse and theories that challenged and toppled the authority of one answer; the system of knowledge has undergone a transformation. Interdiscilinarity has replaced the singularity of approach for knowledge seeking, knowledge generation and knowledge dissemination. Knowledge, in literature is again the wisdom derived through perception, understanding and interpretations of occurrences and accumulated experiences. The relationship between narrative and discourses on human existence is mutually dependent. Literature, through narrative, is capable of creating universal situations and universally applicable understanding of situations. A character, a place, an event described in a novel can seem to have a local flavor and fictitious on the surface but they are universal in its reach and possibilities. Comprising all these essentials as a craftsman with remarkable achievement Amitav Ghosh captures such experiences and characters from real life and infuses them with the creative imagination.

Ghosh is part of the generation of Indian writers in English who were born and brought up in a world where English is relieved of its colonial burden and is not just a medium of expression. His method of narration which keeps on shifting from first person narration to the third person narration is amalgamated with magic realism, linguistic innovations, play with the concept of time, history and digressions—all that make his writings postmodern—reveal his awareness of Indian tradition of narrative techniques. Embellished with high seriousness and experiments, his works are not esoteric. An ability to build up poignancy of a tragedy without succumbing to sentimental descriptions is a unique feature of all his writings. He succeeds in adhering to the form while expressing ideologies and building up snowball like stories. Thus, Ghosh shows a mastery over both Western and Indian Traditions of storytelling. Through his dedication to the world of literature and absolute involvement with the issues of history, subaltern and the issues that engulf the peace of our contemporary world, Ghosh has remained a chief contributor to the world of literature in the second half of twentieth century. He continuous to be a prominent voice even after the arrival of the new generation writers like Kiran Desai, Amit Chaudhary and Arvind Adiga. Human life encompasses multiple roles and multifaceted experiences. As a writer, he tries to represent life with its myriad manifestations. His works transfigures the geographical boundaries and capture the universality of pain and suffering, hope and nobility. The journey that has begun with *The Circle of Reason* after attaining praiseworthy landmarks on the way has come ashore to China with his latest work *River of Smoke*, the second book in the ambitious *Ibis* trilogy. Based on our experience with his past works we may prepare ourselves to see hitherto unexplored aspects of Opium War, some subaltern characters from across the subcontinent, the nuances and the politics of colonialism, the predicament and despair of war, some opportunists exploiting the situation of war in the much awaited third part of the story.

To sum up the issues, ideologies and craftsmanship in Amitav Ghosh's writings, it is evident that his contribution to the world of literature remains of immense importance as he has furthered Indian Writing in English in prose both in terms of content and the form. All his works remain a study of ideological debates on the issues of past and present; penetrating through a complex web of historical, political, economical and the cultural nuances. The oeuvre penned down by him stand for assiduous craftsmanship manifesting his creative contribution to the contemporary world and the humanity in general.

There are some prominent aspects of Ghosh's writings which are unique and worthy of a serious deliberations and worthy of appreciation that this study has discovered but are outside the scope of this work. One such exceptional feature of Ghosh's writings is the amount of research work that he carries out before writing. As the study has discussed, he derives his writings from archival studies, field trips, studying linguistic and cultural histories of the phenomenon and the place he is writing about. It is possible to trace out the research work involved in his writings. Another possible direction for future research is Ghosh's involvement with the merger of topographical and cultural moorings from the cultural studies perspective. Ghosh has set out to make a difference to the usage of English language in fiction. This area is also a potential research to carry out a systematic study of how he has evolved his theory of using English language through all these years.

Working Bibliography

Works by Amitav Ghosh

Ghosh, Amitav. *The Circle of Reason*. 1986. Delhi: Ravi Dayal. 2006. Print.

______. *The Shadow Lines*. 1988. Delhi: Ravi Dayal/Permanent Black. 2006. Print.

______. *In an Antique Land*. 1992. Delhi: Ravi Dayal/Permanent Black. 2006. Print.

______. *The Calcutta Chromosomes*. Delhi: 1996. Ravi Dayal/ Permanent Black. 2006. Print.

______. *Dancing in Cambodia, At Large in Burma*. 1998. Delhi: Ravi Dayal/Permanent Black. 2006. Print.

______. *Countdown*. 1999. Delhi: Ravi Dayal/ Permanent Black. 2005. Print.

______. *The Glass Palace*. 2000. New Delhi: HarperCollins. 2001. Print.

______. *The Imam and the Indian*. 2002. New Delhi: Ravi Dayal/Permanent Black. New Delhi. 2003. Print.

______. *The Hungry Tide*. 2004. London: HarperCollins. London. New Delhi: 2005. Print.

______. *Sea of Poppies*. New Delhi: Viking. Penguin. 2008. Print.

Secondary Works

Books

Arnold, J. *History: A Very Short Introduction*. New York: O.U.P. 2000. Print.

Althusser, L. "Ideology and Ideological State Apparatuses" in *Lenin and Philosophy*. London: New Left Books. 1971. Print.

Ankersmit, F.R. "The Historical Text as Literary Artifact" in *Tropics of Discourse*. Baltimore: John Hopkins University Press. 1973. Print.

Audadkar, Sarita. *Amitav Ghosh: A Critical Study*. New Delhi: Creative Books. 2007. Print.

Barnes, Julian. *Sense of an Ending*. London: Jonathan Cape. 2011. Print.

Bhargava, Rajul (ed.). *Indian Writing in English: The Last Decade*. New Delhi: Rawat. 2002.

Bhatt, Indira and Indira Nityanandm (eds.). *The Fiction of Amitav Ghosh*. New Delhi: Creative Books. 2001. Print.

Bose, Brinda (ed.). *Amitav Ghosh: Critical Perspectives*. Delhi: Pencraft International. 2003. Print.

Bruner, J. *Acts of Meaning*, Cambridge, MA and London: Harvard University Press. 1990. Print.

Cobley, Paul. *Narrative*. 2001. New York: Routledge. 2004. Print.

Chatterjee, Madhuri. "Moving Towards Cultural Periphery: Amitav Ghosh's Dancing in Cambodi, At Large in Burma". *Indian Travel Narratives*. (ed.) Somnath Madal. Jaipur: Rawat Publications. 2010. Print.

Chatterjee, Partha. *The Nation and Its Fragments: Colonial and Postcolonial Histories*, Princeton: Princeton University Press. 1992. Print.

Gandhi, Leela. *A Critical Introduction: Postcolonial Theory*. Edinburgh: Edinburgh University Press. 1998. Print.

Guha, Rnjit (ed.). *Subaltern Studies*, Vol. 1. Delhi: Oxford University Press. 1982. Print.

Dodiya, Jaydipsinh (ed.). *Perspectives on Indian English Fiction*. New Delhi: Dominant. 2002. Print.

Dhawan, R.K. (ed.). *The Novels of Amitav Ghosh*. New Delhi: Prestige Books. 1999. Print.

Eagleton, Terry. *The Ideology of the Aesthetic*. Oxford: 1990. Oxford: Blackwell Publishers. 1994. Print.

Hamilton, Paul. *Historicism*. Oxfordshire.: Routledge. 2007. Print.

Hawley, John. *Amitav Ghosh*. New Delhi : Foundation Books. 2005. Print.

Hoare, Q. and Novell-Smith, G. (ed.). *Prison Notebooks*. A. Gramsci. London: Lawrence and Wishart. 1971. Print.

Kapadia, Novy (ed.). *Amitav Ghosh's The Shadow Lines*. New Delhi: Asia Book Club. 2000. Print.

Khair, Tabish. (ed.). *Amitav Ghosh: A Critical Companion*. Delhi: Permanent Black. 2003. Print.

Jenkins, Kieth. *Refiguring History*. 2003. London: Routledge. 2003. Print.

Lodge, David. *The Art of Fiction*. Harmondsworth: 1992: Penguin. Print.

McLellan, David. *Ideology*. Open University Press: Buckingham and World View Publications: Delhi. 1998. Print.

Meenakshi Mukherjee. *The Perishable Empire: Essays on Indian Writing in English*. New Delhi: Oxford University Press. 2000. Print.

Nayak, M.K. *Indian Writing in English*. 1982. New Delhi: Sahitya Akademi. 2002. Print.

Nayak, M.K., Narayan, Shyamala. *Indian English Literature: 1980-2000—A Critical Survey*. Delhi: Pencraft Intrnational. 2001. Print.

Pandya, Tixita. "A Crtical Study of Amitav Ghosh's Narrative Technique in *The Circle of Reason*, *The Shadow Lines* and *In an Antique Land*" (Unpublished Dissertation). 2010. Print.

Pandey, Gyanendra (ed.). *Subaltern Citizens and Their Histories*. New York: Routledge. 2010.

Rao, Raja. *Kanthapura*. 1938. Delhi: Oxford University Press. 1989. Print.

Ravi, P.S. *Modern Indian Fiction: History, Politics and Individual in the Novels of Salman Rushdie, Amitav Ghosh and Upamanyu Chatterjee*. New Delhi: Prestige Books. 2003. Print.

Schifrin, D. "Narrative as Self Portraits: Sociolinguistic Constructions of Identity". *Language in Soceity*, New York: Rotuledge. 1996. Print.

Therborn, G. *The Ideology of Power and the Power of Ideology*. London: Londn. 1980. Print.

Articles, Interviews

Business Standard, June 21/2008.

Clifford, James. "Looking for Bomma". London Review of Books (24 March 1994):26-27

Dixon, R. "Traveling in The West: The Writing of Amitav Ghosh". *The Journal of Commonwealth Literature*. 31:1. 1996. Print.

Greetz, C. "Ideology as a Cultural System" in *Ideology and Discontent*. (ed.) D. Apter. New York. Free Press. 1964. Print.

Interview EYE, *Sunday Express*, 20 June 2011. Print.

Majeed, Javed. "Amitav Ghosh's *In an Antique Land*: The Ethnographer-Historian and the Limits of Irony". *The Journal of Commonwealth Literature*. 30.2(1995): 45-55

Mukherjee, Meenakshi. "Maps and Mirrors: Coordinates of Meaning in *The Shadow Lines*". *The Shadow Lines*. New Delhi: Oxford University Press. 1995. 255-67.

______. "*In an Antique Lands*". *Indian Review of Books*. 7.10 (1998): 6-8.

Seminar on Amitav Ghosh: A Writer Extra Ordinary, Hooghly. 26 March 2011.

Teltscher, Kate. India/Calcutta: City of Palaces and Dreadful Night. *The Cambridge Companion to Travel Writing*. Peter Hulme and Tim Youngs. (Ed.) 2002. Cambridge: Cambridge University Press. 2008. Print.

Vishwanath, Gauri. "Beyond Orientalism: Syncretism and The Politics of Knowledge". *Stanford Humanities Review*. 5.1 (1995):19-34.

Websites

www.amitavghosh.com

www.asiasource.org/arts/ghosh.cfm

http://www.bbc.co.uk/worldservice

http://www.calcuttaweb.com/articles/lahiri1.htm

http://www.monsoonmag.com/reviews/author_vc.html

www.outlookdindia.com

http://www.youtube.com/watch?v=uNhSy7f_m7g&NR=1&feature=fvwp

Interviews

http://www.bbc.co.uk/programmes/b011tw7z

http://www.listener.co.nz/culture/books/amitav-ghosh-interview/

http://www.untitledbooks.com/features/interviews/amitav-ghosh/

http://onpoint.wbur.org/2011/10/13/amitav-ghosh

http://www.guardian.co.uk/books/2008/jun/07/fiction7

http://www.stumbleupon.com/su/2PYp6q/www.asiasource.org/arts/ghosh.cfm